FINDING FINANCIAL FREEDOM

YOUR KEY

TO DEBT FREE LIVING

D. GREG EBIE

Please feel free to contact me with your questions, comments and ideas. I would also enjoy hearing about your journey to financial freedom.

All communication may be sent to:

D. Greg Ebie, 9815 Nichols Rd. Windham, OH 44288

greg@the firstfaith.com.

ISBN: 10: 1981458735

ISBN-13: 978-1981458738

CONTENTS

INTRODUCTION:

How Will Your Story End?

The Story of Debt

Debt is not a "once upon a time" story. It is unfortunately an all too common story. Debt gives the illusion of a "happily ever after" ending, but with little or no warning our dreams become a nightmare. It's a reality built into the word itself:

D _____

E _____

B _____

T _____ .[1]

> Please note that *Finding Financial Freedom* is intended for you to use as a workbook. You will get more out of this book by personally writing the answers for the fill-in the blanks and completing the worksheets provided. If you are not attending a live seminar or watching it by video, the fill-in answers are included with the footnotes for each page.

Uncontrolled debt is often results from the misuse of credit cards. These two words tell the same acrostic story; your credit card is: *Cravings Realized Enlarge Debt Increasing Tension* and *Cause A Real-life Disaster.*

The purpose of Finding Financial freedom is simple and straightforward. You can rewrite the end of your story. In the following pages, I want to not only share with you the key to financial freedom, but also help you cut your own key and take the necessary steps to achieve financial freedom.

---

[1] Debt Eventually Bring Trouble

notes!

Your financial story does not have to end with trouble, tension and a personal real-life disaster. You can choose to break the chains of debt that are currently holding you and your family hostage. Instead of anxiety and sleepless nights brought on by the unrelenting call of debt collectors and bankruptcy, your story can end with the secret of contentment and a healthy dose of personal peace and liberty. That's financial freedom.

Changing the End of Your Story

Financial _____[2] enables us to see beyond our

current circumstances to a preferable future – a future where we are free from the chains of debt. Solomon said, *"Where there is no vision, the people perish"* (Pro. 29:18 KJV).[3] We need vision to see beyond our present reality of financial hardship. God's desire is for us to be financially free. When we choose to obey the biblical instructions for the financial resources God entrust to us then, *"The LORD your God will bless you as He has promised. You will lend money to many nations but will never need to borrow."* (Deut. 15:6 NLT). God want us to envision His preferable future when we have no need or desire to borrow.

When we lack financial vision to see beyond our current crisis (regardless of how big or small our personal chains of debt might be), we will never live in financial freedom. We must first see it and believe it is possible (see Heb. 11:1). Visionary faith empowers us to find financial freedom as we walk in faithful obedience to the biblical principles in God's Word. In the pages that follow I will share with you the steps you can take to achieve your financial freedom. With the worksheets provided, these steps will help you establish specific financial goals that are measurable and attainable. If you follow these steps many of you will achieve

financial freedom in _____[4] years or less.

My personal financial vision was a simple one – *owe nothing*. My wife and I were tired of working today to pay for the things we had purchased years before. Our vision was drawn from Paul's instruction to the church in Rome: *"Let no debt remain outstanding, except the continuing debt to love one another"* (Rom. 13:8). Today, with the exception of our mortgage, we are blessed to live financially free.

Let me briefly share our story with you because it is my credentials. I'm a graduate from "The School of Hard Knocks." The lessons I've learned have come through trial and error, and I want to help you avoid the pitfalls and financial traps that will continue to bind you in chains of debt.

Footnotes:

[2] Vision

[3] It should be noted that Proverbs 29:18 is better translated: *"Where there is no prophetic vision the people cast off restraint, but blessed is he who keeps the law"* (ESV). The idea Solomon communicated was that without a fresh revelation of God the people will not walk in obedience to His word and are therefore under a curse.

[4] Eight

Our Story to Break the Chains of Debt

My story begins with my parents. I saw them use credit cards. It looked easy; run the card through a machine and take home whatever you wanted. They never taught me that you actually had to pay for those things. Soon after Susie and I were married, my parents lost their house and filed for the first of two bankruptcies. I quickly learned I did not want to follow that path.

Unfortunately, the money lessons we learn as children from our parents are easily lived out as adults. By 1990, I was 28 years old and Susie and I had been married 8 years with three children. But we also had over $25,000 in credit card debt, two car payments and a mortgage. Living from month to month was not enjoyable as we struggled to get by on one income.

I knew if something did not change we were, like my parents, on the path to bankruptcy. That's when I started learning everything I could about financial management. I listened to Larry Burkett on the radio and read his books. As hard as it was we began putting some of the things he taught into practice so we could break free from the chains of debt. While we avoided the pain of bankruptcy we still struggled with debt. By 2008, with five children, we were over $130,000 in debt, much of which was consolidated into our mortgage as the housing market bubble allowed us to borrow more than our house was actually worth. In addition, credit card accounts had been reopened with a running balance of about $18,000. Understand, we were not struggling at that time. We were living comfortably and making our monthly payments on time. Nevertheless, we were still in debt. Clearly my plan was not working as well as I had hoped.

What is Debt?

Before I share the rest of our story, it's important for us to understand what debt really is. Some people think of debt as being financially unable to repay all that is owed. They mistakenly believe that as long as they can make their monthly payments on time, then they are not as they might say, "in debt." Such an attitude shows just how prevalent and acceptable debt is within the American society.

So what is debt? Put simply, debt is an _____. [5]

The dictionary defines debt as "something that is owed or that one is bound to pay to or perform for another."[6] If you have an obligation to repay any amount of money to someone, whether a friend or a financial institution, you are in debt to that individual.

Susie and I knew we were in debt. Even making monthly payments on time, with enough left over to do the things we enjoyed did not change that fact. We owed others more than the continuing

notes!

Footnotes:

[5] Obligation

[6] Debt. http://www.dictionary.com/browse/debt. Accessed, Dec. 12, 2017.

debt of love. That's when I began to apply the principles within *Finding Financial Freedom*. God helped us develop a plan that would enable us to be completely debt free (including paying off our mortgage) by the end of 2015. Sometimes taking these steps were not easy, but we were committed to breaking the chains of debt. I believe we would have reached our goal except we decided in 2013 to buy a new home, which came with a new 15-year mortgage. Our new home is a blessing to our family, and its mortgage was made strategically in light of an unexpected financial lesson my dad taught me.

When Susie and I were first married, my dad encouraged us to buy term life insurance. As a former insurance salesman, he said what you are actually buying is "death insurance" to provide for your family if you are no longer there. He told me that life insurance is often sold with incentives like cash values that can be withdrawn before you die; after all, who really wants to just plan for the day you die? In this way my dad taught me a valuable lesson; term insurance was cheaper than other policies on the market, and the money you saved could be better invested elsewhere. This is sound financial advice, but was regrettably a "do as I say, not as I do" lesson.

In 1986 my dad "fired" me from the family business because he knew that working with him would keep me from pursuing the God's call for me to enter pastoral ministry. He was probably right. Thus from my perception as an outsider looking in, the family business, and in turn my parents, were financially sound. This turned out to not be true. Unexpectedly in September 2012, my dad died. Due to financial pressure he allowed his term life insurance policy to lapse. This left my mom to not only grieve the death of her husband of 52 years, but to also deal with a burden of debt, including a mortgage on their home I though was paid.

This is how suddenly and with little warning my dad taught me an important final financial lesson: be prepared for the day you are no longer there. And so, if paid off according to the bank's terms, I would be 66 years old. I'm working toward paying it off sooner. Yet if something were to happen to my wife or me, our term life insurance will pay it off. You see I've learned that financial

freedom also means not leaving an _____ [7] of debt to those you love.

Today, we enjoy a measure of financial freedom. The decisions we made over the past nine years have broken the chains of recurring debt that held us captive. The *Finding Financial Freedom* plan will put you on a path to eliminate all your debt, but it does something else as well:

It will put you ____ _____ _____ _____ _____,[8]

rather than your money and circumstances dictating how you live. For example, we have enjoyed the freedom to help our children financially, celebrate their weddings without using credit cards, and so much more. Our choice to be financially free also liberated us to follow the Spirit's still small voice in unexpected ways. In 2017, after 19 years as the pastor at Life Church, God directed me to resign from the church we loved. We could not have followed the LORD and launched the ministry of The First Faith except that we made the hard choice to get out of debt and be financially free.

You Decide

You can take our story as a disclaimer if you want, but these principles have worked for my family and me. In the following pages I want to share how to cut the key to your financial freedom. These steps contain sound financial advice from a lifetime of learning and experience. But that's not all. The principles within *Finding Financial Freedom* are more importantly based in scripture. When you apply what the Bible teaches about money to your finances you will discover God's blessings overflowing in your life.

While not given as financial advice, someone said that insanity is doing the same thing over and over but expecting different results. You can let the years go by and keep using money the same way you're spending it now. Time will pass, but you will only be older and still in debt. Or you rewrite the end of your story and choose today to take the necessary steps to be completely debt free. The choice is yours.

It is my prayer that God will help you apply the biblical principles of stewardship to your finances. I believe as you develop your plan, with a commitment to follow it through, that you too will discover the joy of living with financial freedom. So develop your plan and stick with it because in eight years or less you can live life to the fullest and great joy because you will have found financial freedom.

And this is God's plan for you as well. As the LORD spoke to the exiles in Babylon centuries ago, so too God wants you to hear His Spirit whisper a word to your heart. His desire is to bring you out of the captivity of "Babylon," which can be thought of as the oppressive weight of debt holding you captive.

> *"For I know the plans I have for you," declares the LORD, "plans to prosper you and not to harm you, plans to give you hope and a future."* (Jer. 29:11)

God wants you to know that you can be free. You don't have to continue to carry the ball and chain of debt. The LORD gives hope and a future where you can live debt free.

Your Financial Vision

Now that you have heard our story, this would be a good time for you to write how you want your story to end. Prayerfully ask the LORD to show you His desire for the financial resources He has entrusted to you. What will life be like for you to not be dragging around the ball and chain of debt? Take a moment and describe below what financial freedom will look like for you and your family.

THE FIRST STEP:

Biblical Stewardship

THE KEY TO FINANCIAL FREEDOM

A Common Problem

For many Americans living paycheck-to-paycheck is a way of life. It's probably your way of life too. According to an August, 2017 survey:

- 78% of U.S. workers live paycheck-to-paycheck.
- Of those making more than $100,000 per year, one in ten still struggle to make it from one pay period to the next.
- Over 25% of Americans set aside no monthly savings.
- 3 out of 4 workers say they are in debt, and over half believe they will never be debt free.[1]

I believe you are different than most Americans. You have a financial vision to see yourself debt free. More than that your vision is for you and your family to no longer struggle from paycheck to paycheck but to enjoy financial freedom. I have good news.

You can be _____ _____![2]

As the above survey shows the way we handle our money can be a heavy burden for most of us. Many households think they have more month than money. Try as they might they just can't seem to make ends meet. Their struggle is a lot like these folks:

---

[1] Living Paycheck to Paycheck. http://press.careerbuilder.com/2017-08-24-Living-Paycheck-to-Paycheck-is-a-Way-of-Life-for-Majority-of-U-S-Workers-According-to-New-CareerBuilder-Survey, Accessed Dec. 12, 2017

[2] Financially Free

- The man who said, "I never worry about money; I have enough to last me the rest of my life . . . unless I buy something."
- The wife who told her husband, "I've worked out this year's budget. Now you work out the raise."
- The husband who asked his wife for help with the finances, "I think I've got our finances worked out but I need a little help. I've figured what we'll need for food, clothing, the car and housing. We have a choice of any two, so what do you think?"

It's time to change your outlook towards your financial situation. It's time to take hold of your financial vision and believe you can rewrite the end of your story. It's time to take the first step toward financial freedom.

The Glass Jar

Picture in your mind a large glass jar. Now imagine filling the jar with several large rocks until you can't put any more into it. Is the jar full? You might think so, but it's not! If we take a handful of small pea-sized pebbles we can add them to the jar and shake them down into the crevices between the big rocks. Now is the jar full? You've probably already figured out that it's not. We can pour some sand into the jar and watch it fill the remaining gaps. Now the jar is full. Except for you critical thinkers; go ahead and imagine now pouring water into the jar to fill the space between the grains of sand.

What does this illustration teach us? Our minds are like the jar, and they can only hold so much information. You can only fit so many big rocks into the jar, but if you fill the jar with sand first you will never get the big rocks into it. We clutter our minds with a lot of stuff! Some of it is like the sand; it's small and not that important, unless we're spending a day at the beach.

When it comes to money there is a lot that can be said. We can't begin to talk about everything there is to say about finances. What we want to do is to put those big rocks in first and make sure we have

the _____ _____[3] in our minds as a solid foundation.

Biblical Stewardship

Let's be honest; the starting place for many of us means being willing to dump wrong and worthless information out of our minds. We need room for the big ideas that form the foundation for how we think about and in turn handle finances.

The goal of *Finding Financial Freedom* is to help you learn and

Footnotes:

[3] Big Ideas

practice _____ _____.[4] We need to allow the Holy Spirit to renew our minds, so we can _____

_____[5] about money and not like other Americans (see: Rom. 12:2). Biblical stewardship means using our finances in ways that are honoring to God. This is the only way we can establish a foundation of financial freedom in our lives.

Money is a big deal in the Bible! In all over 2,300 verses address the topic of money.[6] This is over four times more than both the 500 verses concerning prayer and less than 500 verses about faith. In Jesus' teaching 16 of His 38 parables deal with money. Within the Gospels, which tell the story of Jesus, 288 verses refer directly to money (that's an amazing one in ten verses).[7]

Why did Jesus talk about money and possessions so much? This is the first and one of the most important lessons we need to learn about the use of our money and possessions because:

_____ _____ _____ ___ __ _____ _____.[8]

The way we think about and handle money is directly connected to our spiritual lives. While we may try to separate our faith and finances, God sees them as inseparable; the two are interconnected with each other. Our attitude and use of money and possessions reveals the real condition of our heart. Notice what Jesus said about our use of money:

> *No one can serve two masters. Either he will hate the one and love the other, or he will be devoted to the one and despise the other. You cannot serve both God and Money.* (Mat. 6:24)

Jesus makes it clear; we cannot divide our affections between God and money. While money is a necessary part of our lives, we must be careful not to let money become the focus of our desires. Jesus said the first and greatest commandment was to love God with

everything within us (see: Mat. 22:37). Money is a _____ _____[9]

that wants to capture our hearts and separate us from the one true God. We should never allow money to become our master; money should be our servant.

Our attitude towards money, and in turn how we use it has the potential to destroy us. Notice Paul's instruction to Timothy:

> *For the love of money is a root of all kinds of evil. Some people, eager for money, have wandered from the faith and pierced themselves with many griefs.* (1 Tim. 6:10)

Footnotes:

[4] Biblical Stewardship

[5] Think Biblically

[6] 2350 Verses on Money. https://www.compass1.eu/2350-verses-on-money/. Accessed, Dec. 13, 2017. This site provides a downloadable list organized by topic as compiled by Mark Lloydbottom.

[7] Statistic: Jesus Teaching on Money. http://www.preachingtoday.com/illustrations/1996/december/410.html. Accessed, Dec. 13, 2017

[8] Every Financial Decision Is A Spiritual Issue.

[9] Rival god

notes!

The Bible does not say that money is evil. Rather, it is the love of money that stirs up evil desires within our hearts. The greater our passion for money and possessions the more likely the rival god of money has become our master. When this happens money becomes a wedge that separates us from God. This is how the root of evil takes hold and grows in our hearts producing a harvest of unrighteousness and sin. Paul says the rival god of money can even lead us away from the faith and our first love for Jesus.

Let's continue to put the foundation of biblical stewardship in place. This idea is contrary to our American culture and won't be easy. But it is a necessary change in thinking. Let the Holy Spirit help

you to _____ _____ _____ _____ _____ _____

____ _____ ____ _____ .[10] Do you know what

the gimmes are? Picture the child crying loudly at the store because mom won't let them have everything their little heart desires. Some of us never out grow the gimmes; we always want more. Credit makes it easy for us to say "Yes" to impulse purchases.

Biblical stewardship has a secret way of thinking – one God wants to help us discover. Notice Paul's testimony:

> *I have learned to be content whatever the circumstances. I know what it is to be in need, and I know what it is to have plenty. I have learned the secret of being content in any and every situation, whether well fed or hungry, whether living in plenty or in want. I can do everything through Him who gives me strength.* (Php. 4:11-13)

Paul has experienced it all – wealth and poverty. But his focus was not on money and the many things it could buy. His desire was not the accumulation of more stuff or the momentary pleasures of wealth because he *"learned the secret of being content in any and every situation."* Can I let you in on the secret Paul learned? The secret of contentment is an unchanging reality based upon a

_____ _____[11] with Jesus Christ. Paul alludes

to the secret of contentment when he says, *"I can do everything through Him who gives me strength."* Contentment is more than just a feeling of satisfaction. True contentment endures regardless of the proverbial ups and downs of life because no matter what may happen, nothing can ever separate us from the love of our heavenly Father (see Rom. 8:31-38).

Footnotes:

[10] Break free from the gimmes with a heart of contentment.

[11] Personal Relationship

14

The secret of contentment teaches us to live life free from the gimmes because satisfaction cannot be obtained by acquiring more and more stuff. This secret is based in the ancient wisdom God gave Solomon:

> *Better a little with the fear of the LORD than great wealth with turmoil.* (Pro. 15:16)

I like how the Message Bible puts this verse: *"A simple life in the Fear-of-God is better than a rich life with a ton of headaches."* The choice is ours. We can peruse the American dream complete with the stress and worry that comes with our pile of stuff, or we can go against the flow and learn the secret of contentment.

Jesus' Story of Biblical Stewardship

We have placed the first two rocks into our jar – the big ideas that form the foundation of biblical stewardship. Jesus' parable of the talents[12] in Matthew 25:14-28 reveals four more big ideas that will further help us think biblically about our finances. It's a familiar story about a rich man who went away on a journey, but before leaving Jesus said he entrusted his wealth to three servants. When their master left the first two servants put the money to work right way, but the third dug a hole and hid his master's money in the ground. When the master finally returned he called his servants to settle accounts. The first reported that he had taken the five talents given to him and doubled it. The second likewise told his master that he had doubled the two talents given to him. But the third dug up his master's wealth and returned it.

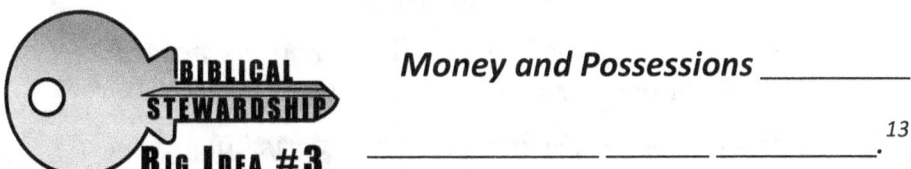

Money and Possessions _____

_____ _____ _____.[13]

The talents did not belong to the servants but to the master. The money and things we call ours do not really belong to us. Everything belongs to God; we are only stewards or managers of that which God has entrusted to us. Paul wrote, *"The earth is the LORD'S, and everything in it"* (1 Cor. 10:26).

King David understood this principle of biblical stewardship. He prepared for the construction of the Temple by giving offerings. Once everything had been brought together David offered up a prayer of thanksgiving to the LORD. Notice what he prayed:

> *Everything in the heavens and on earth is Yours, O LORD, and this is your kingdom. We adore You as the one who is over all things. Wealth and honor come from you alone, for you rule over everything. Power and*

Footnotes:

[12] The Greek word **talanton** often translated "talent" is a measurement of wealth equal to about 200 pounds of gold or 100 pounds of silver. (Talanton. https://www.blueletterbible.org/lang/lexicon/lexicon.cfm?Strongs=G5007&t=NIV. Accessed, Dec. 14, 2017.)

[13] All Belong To God.

might are in your hand, and at your discretion people are made great and given strength . . . Everything we have has come from you, and we give you only what you first gave us! (1 Chr. 29:11-14 NLT)

Everything we consider "_____"[14] does not belong to us.

Biblical thinking always remembers that it all belongs to God. Financial freedom will elude us until this big idea is firmly in our minds. God is the true owner of everything; the LORD has simply loaned it to us to manage for Him.

BIBLICAL STEWARDSHIP

BIG IDEA #4

God Provides _____ _____

_____ _____.[15]

The servants did not receive the same amount. As Jesus said they were given sufficient resources *"each according to his ability"* (v. 15). However, each servant was given enough. Actually, what the master provided was above and beyond the servants' needs. Even the servant given one talent did not use it to buy food or other things for his family. Instead, with his needs already met this lazy servant buried his talent of gold in the backyard to keep it safe.

You and I need this big idea as a foundation in our lives today. The LORD has provided us with enough. Let's put these thoughts in our minds to help us think biblically:

> *And my God will meet all your needs according to his glorious riches in Christ Jesus.* (Php. 4:19)

> *His divine power has given us everything we need for life and godliness.* (2 Pt. 1:3)

You might want to underline this in your thinking. God will always

provide everything we _____; however, the LORD has not

promised to give us everything we _____.[16] The difference between our needs and wants can be as wide and deep as the Grand Canyon, and just as impossible to bring together using our resources. However, if we are going to build biblical stewardship into our lives we must believe that God has provided us with enough to meet all our needs. For many of us, God has done for us just what the master did in Jesus' parable. The LORD has given us more than enough.

Footnotes:

[14] Ours

[15] Enough For Each Servant.

[16] Need, Want

A Servant Must Handle _____

[17]

_____ ____ _____ _____.

notes!

The first two servants immediately went to work and doubled their master's money. The wise servants did not just look at what they had been given, but _____ ____ _____ _____.[18]

With wisdom these servants imagined a preferable future and went to work to make that future dream a reality. The third servant buried his master's money in the ground; he had no vision for the future but lived only for today.

I can't help but imagine how this story might have ended differently. What if the master returned sooner? Instead of doubling their master's money, what if the wise servants were still waiting for the increase? What if the they had nothing except a report of the work they were doing? In Luke's retelling of this parable, he includes an important statement made by the master: *"Put this money to work until I come back"* (Lk. 19:13). The master also imagined what his money could become, which is why he entrusted it to his servants in the first place. I think the master would have still been pleased even if he returned and found his servants still working to increase what had been entrusted to them.

As servants our responsibility is to obey the LORD and trust the outcome to God. Biblical stewardship does not just look at the present, nor will it waste what has been provided. Instead, with wisdom we can be _____ _____.[19] Like the third servant we sometimes live from day to day and spend what we have with little or no thought of tomorrow. We might as well bury bury our talent in the backyard too.

God wants us to plan for the future. Wisdom not only imagines how to increase the wealth entrusted to us, but it also encourages us to prepare financially for the unexpected things that may happen in the months or years ahead. Solomon described it like this:

> *You lazy fool, look at an ant. Watch it closely; let it teach you a thing or two. Nobody has to tell it what to do. All summer it stores up food; at harvest it stockpiles provisions. So how long are you going to laze around doing nothing? . . . Do you know what comes next? Just this: You can look forward to a dirt-poor life, poverty your permanent houseguest!* (Pro. 6:6-8 MSG)

The ant prepares for the future; they arrive at every picnic and carry off everything they can find. But when was the last time you

Footnotes:

[17] The Master's Money Wisely

[18] What It Could Become

[19] Forward Thinking

saw an ant gathering food in the middle of the winter? The ant worked while it could to stored provisions for the future; the ant did not just live for the present but with wisdom made preparation for a later time.

Biblical stewardship prepares for the future. Ask God for wisdom to increase the resources He has provided. Find ways to prepare for the unexpected so you don't have to rely on credit. Continue to have financial vision to work toward the day when you will finally break free from the chains of debt. Biblical stewardship uses wisdom making plans to do the best with what we have while also being "forward thinking" so we are prepared for what yet to come. Let God give you wisdom to use the Master's money wisely.

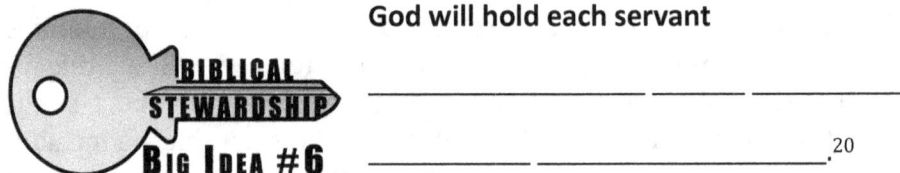

God will hold each servant

_____ _____ _____

_____ _____ .[20]

When the master returned he called in his servants to give a full account for the money they had received. The first two servants both reported how they had doubled their master's money. To each the master replied, *"Well done, good and faithful servant! You have been faithful with a few things; I will put you in charge of many things"* (vv. 21, 25).

The third, however, fearfully returned what he had been given saying, *"I knew that you are a hard man, harvesting where you have not sown and gathering where you have not scattered seed. So I was afraid and went out and hid your gold in the ground. See, here is what belongs to you"* (vv.24-25). This servant was not only foolish, but , Jesus said the master called him a *"wicked, lazy servant"* (v. 26). As a result the master judged him harshly and took away what had been entrusted saying, *"throw that worthless servant outside, into the darkness, where there will be weeping and gnashing of teeth"* (v. 30).

When we stand before the LORD and God opens the books for us to give an account of how we managed the financial resources He entrusted to us, which of these three servants will we be most like? Will Jesus be pleased and entrust us with even more, or will we suffer His wrath? Paul warns us:

> *Yes, each of us will have to give a personal account to God.* (Rom. 14:12 NLT)

We may have been unfaithful with our Master's resources in the

past, but _____ _____ _____ _____ _____ .[21] We can begin

today to be good and faithful servants. God has set a day when we will have to give an account for how we have used what was entrusted to us. Biblical stewardship always remembers that we must give an account to God.

Putting Big Ideas Into Practice

Before we finish this section, let's pause to _____[22] the six big ideas of biblical stewardship to our personal finances. We may agree in theory with these principals; we might even say we have such a foundational way of thinking in our minds. But does what we believe line up with how we handle the financial resources God has placed in our hands?

The ancient Chinese proverb says, *"The journey of a thousand miles begins with the first step."* Let's take that step with an honest evaluation of our financial lifestyle. Ask the Holy Spirit to reveal the true condition of your heart as it relates to your use of money. Only then can we determine if we are actually living out the six big ideas of biblical stewardship.

1. Break free from a _____ _____.[23]

How much of what you make do you spend? The word consumer comes from the word consume, as when a fire consumes what is being burned. Are you "burning money" on an endless buying binge? Even as national credit card debt tops $1 trillion, if you are like most Americans, you don't consider of yourself a consumer. A recent Gallup pole showed that 59 percent of Americans think of themselves as "savers," while only 38 percent say they are "spenders." But according to a GOBankingRates survey of American savings accounts, 34 percent have no savings and another 35 percent have less than $1,000. Retirement savings don't fair much better as nearly half of all Americans have nothing set aside for when they leave the work force.[24] The prophet Jeremiah told us that *"the heart is deceitful above all things"* (Jer. 17:9). Many Americans are not being honest with pollsters – or themselves. Will we admit the truth about our spending habits?

Your Talent of Gold

How much of your _____ _____[25] will you spend, and how much will you save?

Let me ask you another way. Would you have more than enough if I gave you a million dollars? Sure you would right? Wrong! The average wage earner in America will earn between one and three million dollars in their lifetime. The 2016 median personal income for all wage earners was $51,893, which will accumulate $1 million

notes!

Footnotes:

[22] Apply

[23] Consumer Mentality

[24] Emmie Martin, Americans Say They Prefer Saving to Spending . https://www.cnbc.com/2017/05/05/americans-say-they-prefer-saving-to-spending-but-few-actually-follow-through.html. Accessed, Dec. 15, 2017. (Sources were checked to verify this report.)

[25] Lifetime Income

in the next nineteen years – without ever getting a raise![26] We each have the potential to accumulate a great deal of wealth. (See Appendix #1 **"Income in the United States"** to compare your income to national averages—page 61.)

Use the table to calculate your personal lifetime projected income. I've included an example to help. For simplicity I've used gross or pre-tax dollars. Jesus did say, *"Give back to Caesar what is Caesar's,"* so even if we never see that money it counts as income we earned over a lifetime (Mat. 22:21).

1. **Total average annual income since beginning working until now.** Keep in mind this may be lower than your current annual income.	2. **Estimate total annual income from now through retirement.** This will be probably be more than your current annual income:	3. **Estimate total annual retirement income until death.** The Dec. 2016 average SS payment was $1,406.[27] 78.5 years is average U.S. life expectancy. [28]	4. Add up the total for columns 1, 2, and 3. **Estimated total lifetime income.**
Ave. Income: $27,000	$48,000	$19,000	
Multiply # years X 38	X 12	X 11	
$1,026,000	+ **$556,000**	+ **$231,000**	= **$1, 813.000**
Now calculate your estimated total lifetime income:			
			This is your estimated total lifetime income:
	+	+	=

Footnotes:

[26] **Personal Income: 2016.** https://www.census.gov /data/tables/time-series/ demo/income-poverty/ cps-pinc/pinc04.html#par _textimage_12. Accessed Dec. 20, 2017.

[27] **American's Average Social Security Benefit at Age 62.** http://www.foxbusin ess.com/markets/2017/0 1/21/americans-average-social-security-benefit-at-age-62.html. Accessed, Dec. 20, 2017

[28] **Life Expectancy in North America 2017.** https://www.statista.co m/statistics/274513/life-expectancy-in-north-america/. Accessed, Dec. 21, 2017

[29] Exactly How Much

Now ask yourself, *"How much of that money will I keep and how much will I 'burn up' as a consumer?"* You might recall that the master gave five talents, two talents, and one talent to each servant. In ancient Israel, one talent was equivalent to about 200 pounds of gold (see footnote #12, p. 15). At today's values one pound of gold is worth $15,057; that puts the value of a talent of gold at just over $3 million.[25] So what will you do to be a good and faithful servant of the finances God has entrusted to you?

If you're an average wage earner, you might be tempted to think, *"Wow! God has not even trusted me with a talent."* Let me encourage you to not jump to any quick conclusions. Above all don't forget our Master gives to *"each one according to his ability,"* so God knows

_____ _____ _____[29] we can be trusted with (v. 15).

This should not surprise us because employers do the same thing – the higher your education, the greater your annual income. For instance, the 2016 median income for a college graduate was $67,267 compared to only $36,702 for a high school graduate (see Appendix 1). It's also worth pointing out that while we may only estimate our lifetime income, God knows what will be entrusted to us to the penny.

When you and I stop to think about how much wealth has actually been entrusted to us over the course of our lifetimes, it should compel us to want to be a faithful steward of what the LORD has placed into our hands. A life lived with a consumer mentality

does not line up with _____ _____.[30]

Driven by personal ownership, the consumer often believes he does not have enough, or needs newer and better things. Biblical stewardship recognizes that God owns everything and has given it to us as a manager. But that's not all; a biblical stewardship possesses a confident contentment within his heart and is assured that God will always provide enough to meet his needs.

Still think you don't make enough? Most Americans live with a consumer mentality. Why? We have been programmed and taught to spend our money. Even if we have learned biblical stewardship, few of us develop a lifestyle of following biblical principles because other teachers have effectively influenced our thinking to try to live out the elusive "American Dream."

Our _____[31] were our first consumer/credit teachers.

We learned more by the example of our parents, than we ever did at church about financial management. What did you grow up watching your parents do? If you are like me your parents bought things. And how did they buy things: cash, check or charge? Many of us grew up watching our parents use credit, and they never told us how it worked; we just watched them lay down the plastic and bring things home! Now to many of our parent's credit (pun intended), the baby boomers were the first generation to have credit cards. In time these new ways of buying things created a ball and chain of debt few could escape. Now is the time for us to pass on the lessons our parents and we have learned the hard way. Let's teach our children that there is a better way – a path to debt free living.

We really can't blame our parents. Like us, they had powerful teachers encouraging them to live as consumers buying whatever they wanted.

The teachers of _____,[32] the media, merchants, and credit industry were the next to instruct us as consumers.

Advertisers, the media, merchants and the credit industry have created an organized effort to get you to spend as much as you make – and in many cases even more. Collectively they want to siphon off as much of your money as they can. What is important to them is their bottom line — not yours.

Advertisers create desire. Commercials are more about the image and feeling you will have after you bought something, than the information about the product. The media subtly reinforce these messages by showing our favorite stars using the things we think we "need." Merchants line up to make everything" available to us at a special price – but hurry, it's only for a limited time. And credit card companies are right there to make every purchase painless; just sign your name and it can all be yours. We have learned their lessons well. Our homes and garages are full of things we rarely use, and our mailbox is filled regularly with bills to pay for everything we have accumulated.

"_____ _____" [33] **drive home the consumerism lessons boasting about all the things they buy.**

If what we learn from our parents, the advertisers and media is not enough to get us to take the bait of the merchants and credit industry, then there is one more powerful teacher: "the Jones." Everyone wants to *"keep up with the Jones!"* Whatever the Jones buy unconsciously puts extreme pressure on us to do the same. You are responsible for your life and the Jones are responsible for theirs. Choose your goal, not theirs!

2. Break free from the endless cycle of purchasing things

with _____ [34]*.*

The simple truth is credit purchases are less painful – the same is true for debit cards. And with the advent of the electronic wallet included on your cell phone payment becomes even easier. The less pain we feel results in spending more. Restaurants report larger tips from patrons using plastic over a cash payment option. Another study showed that people were willing to pay twice as much for basketball tickets when told they would pay with a credit card over those told they would have to pay with cash. When we use cash or a

check to make a purchase we feel ____ _____ ____ _____.[35]

As a result we not only spend less, but we also make wiser purchasing decisions. Those using plastic to buy groceries load up on more junk food than those using cash. Credit makes impulse buying easy.[36]

Take the following credit quiz:

❑ Yes ❑ No – Are you living from month-to-month and paycheck-to-paycheck?

❑ Yes ❑ No – Are you carrying a balance on one or more credit cards?

❑ Yes ❑ No – Are you just making the minimum payments on any of your credit card balances?

Footnotes:
_____

[20] The Jones

[34] Credit

[35] A Sense of Loss

[36] **Going Shopping? How You Pay Can Effect How Much You Spend.** https://www.consumerreports.org/shopping-retail/how-you-pay-can-affect-how-much-you-spend/. Assessed. Dec. 21. 2017.

❑ Yes ❑ No – Do you buy groceries with a credit card?

❑ Yes ❑ No – Do you use a credit card or cash advance to pay bills?

❑ Yes ❑ No – Have you used a balance transfer option, or home equity loan to try to get a handle on your finances in the past two or three years?

❑ Yes ❑ No – Do you have a car loan or lease?

❑ Yes ❑ No – Do you have a second car loan or lease?

❑ Yes ❑ No – Have you considered or already filed for bankruptcy?

❑ Yes ❑ No – Do finances cause you stress or make you lose sleep?

❑ Yes ❑ No – Have you added an electronic wallet or other payment options to your smart phone?

❑ Yes ❑ No – Do you use a credit or debit card to make purchases online?

❑ Yes ❑ No – Do you use credit cards to earn "cash back" or other reward incentives?

❑ Yes ❑ No – Do you often take advantage of "same as cash" or other "zero interest" offers on major purchases?

❑ Yes ❑ No – Do you and your spouse fight about money?

With every question you answered yes, the greater your financial bondage. Every yes answer is another link in the chain that holds you captive. Purchase by purchase, debt by debt, you are building a financial prison where you are the prisoner. Solomon understood this reality:

> *The rich rule over the poor, and the borrower is servant to the lender.* (Pro. 22:7)

You're looking for freedom but can't seem to find a way out because each credit purchase tightens the control of the lender over you. The key to unlock the chains of your financial prison is to stop using credit – period.

The time has come for you to go against the flow and decide to be free from the burden of debt. You can find financial freedom for you and your family as you stop chasing the Jones and buying with credit. It's not too late for you to begin to teach your children biblical stewardship. More lessons are "caught" than "taught." Your children, and even grandchildren, will see you take responsibility for the resources God entrusts to you. And one day soon, they will do the same as a good and faithful servant.

Do you know what using credit cards _____ _____[37] you?

Making a purchase with a credit card is easy, so easy we seldom stop to think about how it actually affects the cost of what we buy. Our only thought is can we afford to make the monthly payment. And that's how the credit card companies want us to think because that's how they get rich.

Footnotes:

[37] Really Costs

notes!

Let's say you have $2,500 on a credit card. It might be from a single purchase for something like a large screen TV, or maybe it was taking the kids shopping for back-to-school. The typical minimum monthly payment would be 2% or $50 a month. That's not much for a new TV or sending the kids back-to-school in style! But if you only make the minimum monthly payment, you will pay

_____ _____ _____,[38] than what you paid for your

original purchase. With an 18% interest rate it would take you 28 years to pay it off making just the minimum monthly payment. You would add a $5,897 in interest to your original $2,500 purchase for a total cost of $8,397. The real difficulty is that few of us actually pay off our credit cards, but have a continual revolving door of credit.[39]

When we apply the six principles of Biblical stewardship in our day-to-day lives, we sill use financial resources wisely. With wisdom

we will _____ _____ _____[40] of buying with credit and

understand how credit purchases can negatively affect our long-term goals.

3. Break free from being a _____ with the _____ of dissatisfaction.[41]

Some folks will blame anyone and everyone for their problems!

We all remember the phrase, "It's the economy, stupid." It was made famous by political strategist James Carville, hanging it in Bill Clinton's Little Rock campaign office to keep everybody "on message" in the 1992 election. And it worked: Clinton won the election over George Bush senior, who was soaring in the polls after winning the war in Iraq. Little has changed since then; people still blame various politicians for the financial woes we face.

While politicians may try to win elections by focusing on "the

economy," _____ _____[42] is far more important. How is

your economy? As you apply the six principles of Biblical stewardship, you will take responsibility for your personal finances. Biblical stewards do not blame politicians, where they live, or anything else for their financial condition. Your economy is the result of your personal financial decisions—period!

Here is the simple truth. Only as you take responsibility for your

economy will you then have _____ _____.[43] If you

only want to blame others for why you are experiencing financial difficulty, then you will never have the ability to do anything about your financial condition. You will always be hoping someone or

Footnotes:

[38] More In Interest

[39] **The True Cost of Credit Cards.** https://www.thebalance.com/the-true-cost-of-credit-cards-1289627. Accessed, Dec. 21, 2017

[40] Count The Cost

[41] Crybaby, Complaints

[42] Your Economy

[43] Response Ability

something will change things for you. Unfortunately, no one ever comes to your rescue! However, taking responsibility empowers you to make needed changes with response ability.

Your Foundation of Biblical Stewardship

So how established are the six big ideas of biblical stewardship in your mind as a solid foundation? Biblical stewardship is the key to your financial freedom. Before moving on to cut your personal key to financial freedom, take a few moments and review the six big ideas. What needs to change in your thinking so these principles become the foundation for the way you will handle your money so you can break free from the chains of debt?

Which of the six big ideas of biblical stewardship do you find most challenging? Why?

It's time for action. How will you apply the principles of biblical stewardship?

THE SECOND STEP:

Unlocking Your Finances

CUTTING YOUR KEY TO FINANCIAL FREEDOM

What Is Financial Freedom?

Now that we have established a foundation of biblical stewardship, let's draw our target of financial freedom so we know exactly what we are shooting at. This is an important first step.

Perhaps you have heard the story of Charlie Brown shooting arrows and then drawing a circle around each arrow? When Linus asked what he was doing, Charlie Brown responded, *"This way I never miss!"* Sometimes we are just like that; when you shoot aimlessly you can't miss. However, if we are going to hit the target of financial freedom, we must first draw the circle to know what we are shooting at, then take aim at a target and let the arrow fly! While we may initially miss our target, with God's help each shot will be closer to the mark. Little by little, and with steady perseverance, we will hit the target and achieve our goal of financial freedom.

If we are not careful, you and I could find ourselves shooting at the wrong target. Many Americans think financial freedom is obtained with greater wealth. We would be wise to take some advice from one of the wealthiest men in modern history. John D. Rockefeller said, *"If your only goal is to become rich, you will never achieve it."*[1] He understood that wealth was elusive; perhaps he was familiar with the Wisdom of Solomon:

> **Whoever loves money never has money enough; whoever loves wealth is never satisfied with his income. This too is meaningless.** (Ecc. 5:10)

An ever-increasing stockpile of more money and possessions is the wrong target because no matter how much you have you always want more. Jesus told a story about such a rich man saying:

---

[1] **30 Inspirational John D. Rockefeller Quotes On Success.** http://awakenthegreatnesswithin.com/30-inspirational-john-d-rockefeller-quotes-success/. Accessed, Dec. 27, 2017. (His net worth adjusted for inflation at the time of death $340 billion)

notes!

A rich man had a fertile farm that produced fine crops. In fact, his barns were full to overflowing. So he said, "I know! I'll tear down my barns and build bigger ones. Then I'll have room enough to store everything. And I'll sit back and say to myself, 'My friend, you have enough stored away for years to come. Now take it easy! Eat, drink, and be merry!'"

But God said to him, "You fool! You will die this very night. Then who will get it all?" Yes, a person is a fool to store up earthly wealth but not have a rich relationship with God. (Lk. 12:16-21 NLT)

Jesus was direct and to the point; our lives are more than money. God calls the person who thinks only of accumulating more and more

wealth for himself "_____ _____."[2]

An Example to Follow

It has been said, *"A picture is worth a thousand words."* I think we can better understand how God describes financial freedom by looking at the example of the Early Church. We share a common faith in Christ with these first century believers, but how their faith impacted their use of their money and possessions is foreign to most of us. Here is how Luke tells their story:

All the believers were one in heart and mind. No one claimed that any of their possessions was their own, but they shared everything they had. With great power the apostles continued to testify to the resurrection of the LORD Jesus. And God's grace was so powerfully at work in them all that there were no needy persons among them. For from time to time those who owned land or houses sold them, brought the money from the sales and put it at the apostles' feet, and it was distributed to anyone who had need. (Act. 4:32-35)

So what does this short story teach us about what financial freedom means for you and me as followers of Jesus?

1. *Financial freedom demonstrates* _____[3]
with what God provides.

Can you see the contentment of these first century believers? God gives us a glimpse into their hearts and shows us how they freely *"shared everything they had,"* rather than hording things as their own. They were living out what Paul called *"the secret of being content"* (Php.4:12). The American economy does not offer such fulfillment. We only learn this secret with confidence of God our

Footnotes:

[2] A Fool

[3] Contentment

28

Father's unfailing provision for us. We can join in singing this ancient song of praise:

> *No good thing does He withhold from those who walk uprightly. O LORD of hosts, blessed is the one who trusts in You!* (Ps. 84:11-12 ESV)

Such confidence does not come from our good works; righteousness cannot be earned. It is only by faith in Christ that we receive the abundant blessing of God's loving provision. It is then that we know that the LORD will meet our every need, and we will lack nothing.

The Apostle Paul further helps us understand God's provision and the secret of contentment in what he wrote to Timothy:

> *But godliness with contentment is great gain. For we brought nothing into the world, and we can take nothing out of it. But if we have food and clothing, we will be content with that.* (1 Tim. 6:6-8)

God has given us far more than just food and clothing. Let's learn the secret of contentment, satisfied with the abundance of all that God has given to us.

2. *Financial freedom* _____ ____ _____ *and* _____ [4]
   with those in need.

Like the toddler who grabs a toy and cries, *"Mine!"* we are quick to think only of ourselves. The attitude of those in the Early Church was different. These believers were united *"one in heart and mind"* aware of the needs of others, so much so *"that there were no needy persons among them."* Thinking of others to provide for their need is the overflow of a heart of contentment.

Everything God gives us should be held in an open hand and not a clenched fist. These believers freely shared with others because they understood that in God's economy there is always enough for everyone. Consider Paul's instruction to the believers in Corinth:

> *At the present time your plenty will supply what they need, so that in turn their plenty will supply what you need. The goal is equality, as it is written: "The one who gathered much did not have too much, and the one who gathered little did not have too little."* (2 Cor. 8:14-15)

God's blessing upon our financial resources is not just for us to enjoy; it is entrusted to us to share with others. I think the scriptures further teach us how to prioritize our giving to help provide for the

needs of others: (1) _____, (2) the _____,

and lastly (3) the _____. [5]

29

Footnotes:

[4] Thinks Of Others, Shares

[5] Family, Church, Community

3. Financial freedom remains _____ _____[6] by making purchases with cash and not credit.

I think the Luke's choice of words to describe how believers in the Early Church met the needs of others is significant. He tells us *"from time to time those who owned land or houses sold them."* He does not say they gave the proceeds from the sale of mortgaged land or houses, nor was provision being made by credit. Rather, he specifically says they laid money at the Apostles' feet from the sale of property they owned.

Perhaps you think this is an unrealistic goal. It is possible for you to not only pay off your credit card debt, but to also pay off your car loans and your mortgage using the income you presently make. How do we know this is true? Think about one thing every credit application you ever completed shares in common with the others. Each requires the disclosure of your personal income. Banks and lenders will not let you borrow more than they believe you can repay.

The LORD wants you to live financially free. God does not want His children to be bound by the chains of debt. Notice His promise to those who follow His instructions and obey His commands:

> *The LORD will open the heavens, the storehouse of his bounty, to send rain on your land in season and to bless all the work of your hands. You will lend to many nations but will borrow from none.* (Deut. 28:12)

God wants to bless His children and enable us to have all of our needs met through His abundant supply.

4. The final benefit of financial freedom is having the ability

to _____ _____.[7]

Building wealth is not the primary goal of finding financial freedom. Remember Solomon's Wisdom (and Rockefeller's advice); those who start here are *"never satisfied with his income. This too is meaningless"* (Ecc. 5:10). If you make wealth your first goal you will always be in financial bondage – always longing for more, even if you succeed and become wealthy beyond your wildest dreams. More than that, you are also in bondage to sin because *"the love of money is a root of all kinds of evil"* (1 Tim. 6:10).

How does the example of the Early Church reveal this principle? We have to continue the story; one you are most likely familiar with. Luke ends Acts 4 telling of man called Barnabas who sold a field he owned and placed the money at the feet of the Apostles. The next chapter begins with the story of Ananias and Sapphira who followed

Footnotes:

[6] Debt Free

[7] Build Wealth

Barnabas' example. They too sold a field, but they decided to lie about the price and keep some of the money for themselves. Their sin was not keeping some for themselves, but lying to deceive others into thinking that they too had freely given. This lie cost them their lives. The key to building wealth is found in what Peter said:

> *Ananias, how is it that Satan has so filled your heart that you have lied to the Holy Spirit and have kept for yourself some of the money you received for the land? <u>Didn't it belong to you before it was sold? And after it was sold, wasn't the money at your disposal?</u> What made you think of doing such a thing? You have not lied just to human beings but to God.* (Act. 5:3-4)

God had entrusted the land, and the money form the sale, to Ananias and Sapphira to use as they wanted. Unfortunately they chose to lie, not only to the Apostles, but to God as well. Their deceit shows that they were not content but doubted God's provision for them. Instead of thinking of others they were more concerned with what people in the church would think about them – their pride motivated them to be thought of as generous.

Now don't miss this point – God is not opposed to the rich. The LORD can and will enable you to increase your net worth and grow your personal bottom line. However, with wealth comes an even greater test of our commitment to serve God with our finances.

> *Beware lest you say in your heart, 'My power and the might of my hand have gotten me this wealth.' You shall remember the LORD your God, for it is he who gives you power to get wealth.* (Deut. 8:17-18)

The greater your wealth, the easier it is to forget the LORD. God does not want wealth to control our lives and become our first priority – a false and rival god. Instead we are to keep the LORD first and faithfully manage all that God entrusts to us. Wealth should not be your primary goal lest you fail the test and money leads you astray.

It is important for us to keep the target of financial freedom clearly in view. Financial freedom:

- Demonstrates _____.

- Thinks of _____ sharing to meet their needs.

- Remains _____ _____ using cash and not credit.

- Builds _____[8] but keeps the LORD first.

The American financial priorities we grew up with are contrary to this target and make it difficult to keep the target of financial freedom based upon Biblical stewardship in view. Luke tells us what

Footnotes:

[8] Contentment, Others, Debt Free, Wealth

made it possible for the first century believers saying, ***"God's grace was so powerfully at work in them all"*** (Act. 4:33). The grace of God is both the cause and effect of true financial freedom. With the story of the Early Church and the grace of God upon them in mind, King Agur provides us with a prayer that will help us keep the target of financial freedom clearly in view.

> ***Keep falsehood and lies far from me; give me neither poverty nor riches, but give me only my daily bread. Otherwise, I may have too much and disown you and say, "Who is the LORD?" Or I may become poor and steal, and so dishonor the name of my God.*** (Pro. 30:8-9)

More than being a prayer of financial freedom, Agur's is a prayer of integrity. Two ways we will be recognized as a person of Godly character is through what we say and do. Will our words and deed with regard to money provide evidence of our righteousness in Christ Jesus our LORD?

> Look back at your financial vision – the preferable future you described of being debt free. Does what you wrote line up with the target of financial freedom grounded in biblical stewardship? Now is the time for you to further clarify your target of financial freedom (see p. 10).

Cutting The Key to Unlock Your Finances.

Just as a locksmith cuts a key to open a lock, we want to cut a key to financial freedom. Your key will have seven notches or action steps. Don't shortcut any of these steps. If a locksmith miss cuts a key, the lock will not open. Likewise, if you neglect any of the seven notches in your financial freedom key, you will find yourself frustrated and unable to unlock the chains of debt keeping you from financial freedom.

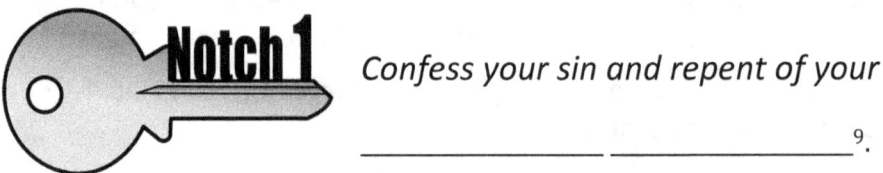

Notch 1 *Confess your sin and repent of your*

_____ _____ [9].

The starting point is to come into agreement with God. Your financial mess is not the result of "the economy." Your house is not in financial turmoil just because of poor planning or bad decisions on your part. If you are have not followed the principles of biblical stewardship, then you have sinned against God. You might like to just call it a mistake, but because every financial decision is a spiritual issue you need to agree with God about your sin.

Repentance is the first step in taking responsibility for your economy. True repentance is more than just telling God, "I'm sorry;"

Footnotes:

[9] Financial Disobedience

it's more than saying, "God forgive me." That's just the beginning. Repentance is to do an about-face. Instead of following your own path, you turn toward God with a commitment to obey His word. In regard to your finances, repentance means looking to the LORD to help you follow the principles of stewardship established in His Word.

Here's the good news. God will not leave you in the mess you have made. Notice what Peter told those who were cut to the heart because of their sin against God:

> *Repent, then, and turn to God, so that your sins may be wiped out, that times of refreshing may come from the LORD.* (Act. 3:19)

I like how the Message Bible expresses this promise: *"Now it's time to change your ways! Turn to face God so He can wipe away your sins, pour out showers of blessing to refresh you."* As we change direction God will forgive and pour out His blessing in our lives.

I know many Christians who have struggled with their finances. They have prayed and asked God for wisdom; they wanted the LORD'S blessing on their finances. The truth is, I have prayed like that. Unfortunately, many have seen things only seem to go from bad to worse. In time some even want to blame God for their problems. The issue was not their faith, but a willingness to repent of their sin.

Don't expect the LORD to do for you by miracle what He will only do

through _____ and _____.[10]

Confession brings about a change of heart so we can begin to learn the secret of contentment. Repentance changes our direction so we can begin to follow God's plan of Biblical stewardship for the proper use of money and financial resources.

REPENTANCE ACTION STEP: _____ _____ your credit cards.[11]

With every temptation God will give us a way of escape (see: 1 Cor. 10:13). You are only setting yourself up for failure if you hold onto credit cards. Would you go on a diet and keep cake, ice cream, and your other favorite snacks around the house? Of course not!

The best way for you to begin to live by biblical principles and stop making new debt is to get rid of the credit cards. As long as you hold on to them it will be too easy to fall back into old habits and make unwise decisions.

If you think you need to hold onto one credit card in the event of an emergency, then seal it in an envelope and give it to your pastor or someone you trust to hold for you. Don't keep it in your wallet or around the house; otherwise new school clothes or dinner at your favorite restaurant may be your "emergency."

notes!

Footnotes:

[10] Repentance, Obedience

[11] Cut Up

Cut the first notch in your key toward financial freedom. Say this prayer aloud:

> LORD, I confess that I have not managed my finances as You desire. Forgive me and give me a fresh start. I believe that You will set me free from the bondage of debt and set me free to live on an all-cash basis. Help me, LORD, to be disciplined and achieve the goal of being truly financially free. Forgive me for trying to find satisfaction in the things of this world. I know my contentment is found in You and not in money or things. With your help, I will be content and completely satisfied with what You provide for me and my family. LORD, with Your help I will hold everything You give me in an open hand; I will not think only of myself, but because You have set me free I will share from the abundance of Your supply with those in need. Help me to keep Jesus Christ first in my heart and not make money my god. As You enable me to one day build wealth, keep me free from the bondage of sin and greed. Thank You, LORD for setting me free!

Thank God _____[12] with joy for His provision and help.

VeggieTales'® Madam Blueberry learned that satisfaction could not be purchased at Stuff-Mart because *"a thankful heart is a happy heart."* Thanksgiving helps develop a heart of contentment confident that God will always meet our needs.

The world in which we live will easily distract us and entice us to chase the American dream. Daily thanksgiving keeps our focus on God's loving provision. Thankfulness will also help us not make impulse purchases with the hope of happiness. Look what Paul said:

> *I'm just as happy with little as with much, with much as with little. I've found the recipe for being happy whether full or hungry, hands full or hands empty . . . You can be sure that God will take care of everything you need, His generosity exceeding even yours in the glory that pours from Jesus.* (Php. 4:12, 19 MSG)

Our joy and happiness is found in the LORD and not things. Is it any wonder that even from prison Paul would encourage us repeatedly to express thanksgiving with joy at all times? Therefore let us:

> *"Rejoice in the LORD . . . Rejoice in the LORD always. I will say it again: Rejoice! . . . in every situation, by prayer and petition, with thanksgiving, present your requests to God."* (Php. 3:1; 4:4)

Footnotes:

[12] Everyday

Notch 3 *Walk in financial obedience as you*

_____ _____[13] *of your income to the LORD through your local church.*

notes!

Don't short cut this step! Some people say, *"I can't afford to tithe."* What they are really saying is, *"I don't trust God; therefore I can't afford to obey God."* A heart of contentment overflowing with joyful thanksgiving empowers you to trust God and obey His word.

We might say we believe in tithing, but few of us actually give 10% or more of our income. According to research by the Barna Group, only 5% of all adults tithed in 2012. Tithing rates are only slightly higher among those who consider themselves born again Christians at 12%, a number consistent for the past decade.[15]

God has much to say regarding the tithe in the scriptures, in both the Old and New Testaments, far more than we have time for here. Let's focus our attention on just one passage. The LORD speaks in Malachi 3:6-12 to His people about the tithe, so let's ask the Holy Spirit to give us ears to hear what God has said.[14] Within these seven verses are at least four lessons the Holy Spirit wants to teach us about the tithe.

1. The LORD calls us to return to Him in _____

assured of His _____.[16]

God does not change, so His people *"are not destroyed"* (v. 6). In mery the LORD says, ***"Return to me, and I will return to you"*** (v. 7); God calls out for them to repent of their sin. This too is our starting place, the first notch in our key. We must return to God in repentance and receive His mercy.

2. The tithe _____to God and is not ours to keep; we are

guilty of _____ against the LORD when we don't give it.[17]

The LORD asks, ***"Will a mere mortal rob God? Yet you rob me ... In tithes and offerings"*** (v. 8). Witholding the tithe as our own makes us a theif; we have stolen God's property. God's indictment against those who do not give the tithe should not surprise us. Big idea #3 of Biblical stewardship has been placed within our thinking; we know that <u>everything belongs to the LORD</u>. It's not just the tithe or 10% of our income that belongs to God, the other 90% is the LORD'S as well.

3. Keeping the tithe for ourselves puts us under a _____.[18]

The LORD tells us plainly, ***"You are under a curse ... because you are robbing me"*** (v. 9). The many links in our chain of debt is

Footnotes:

[13] <u>Tithe 10%</u>

[14] Some might argue Malachi's message does not apply today because it was written to the priests of Israel. Even if this was the case, it still applies to us as believers today because we are chosen by God to serve as *"a royal priesthood"* (1 Pt. 2:9).

[15] **American Donor Trends.** https://www.barna.com/research/american-donor-trends/. Accessed, Dec. 28, 2017.

[16] <u>Repentance</u>, <u>Mercy</u>

[17] <u>Belongs</u>, <u>Robbery</u>

[18] <u>Curse</u>

notes!

evidence of God's curse upon us. Our financial bondage cannot be broken as long as the curse remains.

God's blessing will never be upon our finances as long as we refuse to give the tithe. The choice is ours to make – a choice between

_____ and _____.[19] We can remain under a curse, or we can choose instead to give the tithe to its rightful owner, the LORD. Don't waste your time asking God to bless you financially if you are not willing to obey His Word. Let's face it; if you have not been tithing then the financial mess you are in is one of the consequences of disobedience. Now do you want to try to solve your money madness on your own, or do you want God's blessing upon your finances to help you find financial freedom? The choice is yours – will you obey God or not?

4. Obedience in giving the tithe brings the LORD'S _____.[20]

The LORD says, *"Test me in this"* (v. 10). This amazes me; it is as though the God is daring us to obey and give the tithe. The LORD challenges us to obedience because God wants to bless us. The Almighty continues saying, *"see if I will not throw open the floodgates of heaven and pour out so much blessing that there will not be room enough to store it"* (v. 10). With obedience we won't be able to contain the overflow of God's blessings in our lives.

One such blessing is how tithing affects how we handle money in every area of our lives. Tithing reminds us of two important truths: (1) every financial decision is a spiritual issue, and (2) everything belongs to God. These reminders strengthen our desire to please the LORD with the day-to-day choices we make when spending money.

(For more see: Appendix #2 "Living Giving Principles" page 62)

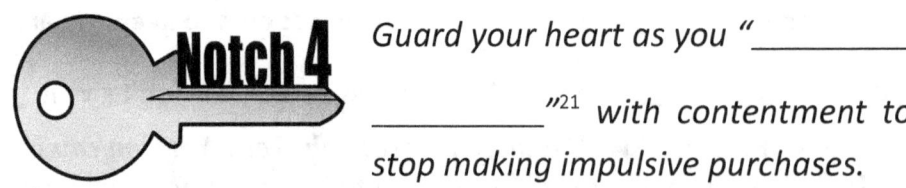 *Guard your heart as you "_____ _____"[21] with contentment to stop making impulsive purchases.*

Before making a purchase we need to "step back" and look at it in light of our financial vision. Every choice we make, and every dollar we spend impacts our ability to achieve the goal of financial freedom set before us. Paul said:

> *Don't be misled. Remember that you can't ignore God and get away with it. You will always reap what you sow!* (Gal. 6:7 NLT)

It is simple cause and effect. The spending choices we make today will either reap a harvest of continued financial bondage or lead to financial freedom tomorrow. So what should we do?

Footnotes:

[19] Obedience, Disobedience

[20] Blessings

[21] Step Back

"Step Back" and learn to _____ _____ _____
_____.[21]

Every purchasing decision is important regardless of how big or small it may see. The decisions we make before we get to the cash register pave the way to financial freedom. Before making any purchase we remember our decision to always pay with cash and not use credit. However, we also need to stop and think about what we buy.

"Step back" and don't be impulsive about the things you buy – <u>think first</u>! We will fine-tune the cutting of this notch with some practical steps to help you think about your purchase decisions and find the money you have been wasting in the next chapter.

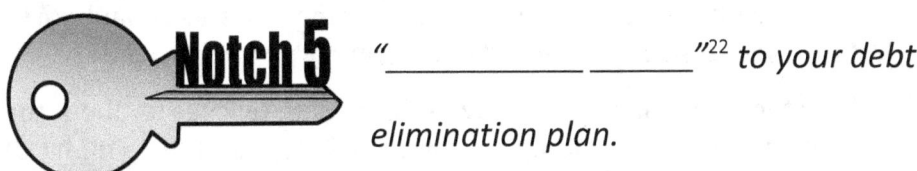 **Notch 5** "_____ _____"[22] *to your debt*

elimination plan.

Your "step-up" plan will empower you to have real financial freedom! While it might be difficult for you to see right now, a debt elimination plan is a necessary notch in your key to financial freedom. Trust me; I know that you are willing to follow your plan you can free yourself from the bondage of debt with your current income.

Remember, we are not just talking about eliminating your credit

card debt; we are going to eliminate _____ _____:[23] **mortgages,**

car payments, personal loans, etc. The idea of paying off all your debt might sound too good to be true. But you can do it! You will be amazed how quickly you can be set free from the bondage of debt.

Imagine lining all your debts up like tin cans on a split rail fence. If you throw a hand full of rocks at the cans you might knock a few of them onto the ground, but the most would still be sitting on the fence. But what would happen if you took the same handful of rocks and placed one rock at a time in a slingshot? Before long you will have hit the target and knocked all the cans off the fence.

Your "step-up" plan will help you do the same thing to your debts. Instead of just "throwing money" at your debts, you will learn how to take aim and pay off each debt following an organized plan. Don't worry if you can't see how this will work right now. This fifth notch vital to your financial freedom. In the next chapter the "step-up" debt elimination plan will be developed with some hands-on advice how you can make it work for you.

Footnotes:

[21] Think Before You Buy

[22] Step Up

[23] All Debt

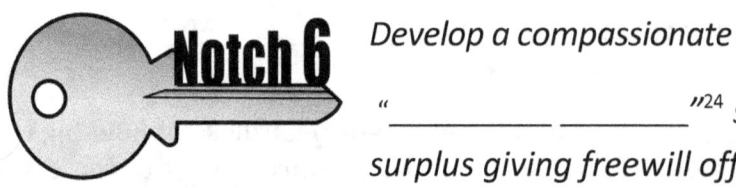

Develop a compassionate heart as you

"_____ _____"[24] *sharing your surplus giving freewill offerings.*

If we are to find financial freedom, we must allow the Holy Spirit to help us overcome the fear that we will not have enough. Our problem is we look at the wrong data. Or put another way, we only see what adds up according to the world's economy. When we only look at the dollars and cents in our bank account, we will never think we have enough to share with others.

We need to allow God to give us supernatural insight into His promises. With eyes of faith see and believe that the LORD will always provide enough. We can enjoy God's blessing because we are walking in obedience by giving the tithe and offerings. As Paul said, *"My God will meet all your needs"* (Php. 4:19).

The story of Elijah and a widow in Zarephath teaches us about the abundance of God's economy is (see: 1 Kings 17:7-16). In the midst of three years of famine, her cupboard was bare. She had enough flour and oil to prepare one last loaf of bread for her and her son to eat; then they would just wait to die. That's when Elijah asked her to fix a meal for him first. Maybe she thought she had nothing to lose, so she emptied her jars and made the bread for Elijah. But where she saw nothing more, God saw more than enough to provide for more than a year: *"the jar of flour was not used up and the jug of oil did not run dry, in keeping with the word of the LORD"* (1 Kg. 17:16).

God will provide enough to meet our needs – sometimes with more than enough. Even as we pay off our debts, God can direct us to share with others or to give freewill offerings for special ministries or missionaries. Compassion for the needs of others compels us to action, and produces generosity in giving.

When we close our fists tightly around a handful of sand we always have less. Keep your hand open because there is always room for more when our heart is willing to share with others. God's economy is not our economy. The LORD will always supply enough.

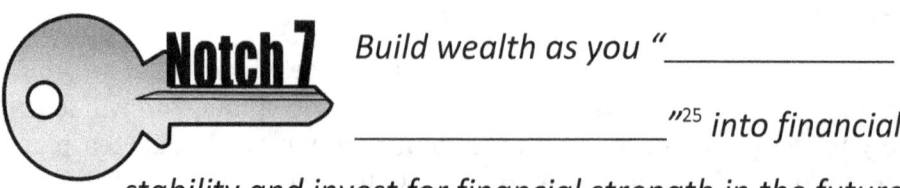

Build wealth as you "_____

_____"[25] into financial

stability and invest for financial strength in the future.

You might think this notch cannot be cut until you are debt free. Actually, you begin to build wealth each month as you follow your debt elimination plan. Your wealth (what accountants call your net worth) is the difference between what you own (your assets) and

Footnotes:

[24] Step Out

[25] Step Forward

notes!

what you owe (your liabilities). A simple balance sheet will help you see how you are wealthier as you pay off your debts.

Where You Started		After One Month		
Total Assets The value of your house, cars, etc. plus the cash you have in checking and savings.	$219,891.^{00}	**Net Income** The difference between your monthly income and total bills and expenses.	$ -101.^{00}	**Total Assets** $219,790.^{00}
Total Liabilities Everything you owe: mortgage, car loans, credit cards etc.	$-215,537.^{00}	**Debt Payments** Minimum payments plus your "step up" payment.	$2,992.^{00}	**Total Liabilities** $-212,545.^{00}
Net Worth The difference between assets and liabilities.	$ 4,354.^{00}	**Net Worth** Your bottom line after one month shows that you are wealthier.		$ 7,245.^{00}

In the above example, your total assets decreased at the end of the month because you had a negative net worth. This could be because you had an unexpected expense (one of the kids got sick, or you had a flat tire). But instead of using a credit card, you paid for this with cash from your savings account. You might feel "poorer" because you have less money in savings, but notice what happened to your net worth. Because you followed your step up debt elimination plan and did not use credit, your net worth increased $2,891.^{00}; you are richer at the end of the month than you were when it started.

The second way you step forward to build wealth is to _____

_____ _____.[26]

Now is the time to intentionally begin saving money. Remember, if you are like most Americans you have less than $1,000 in savings account. You need to pay yourself first and include in your monthly budget how much you will set aside. Think of this as your "emergency fund;" you need to prepare for the unexpected so you don't have to fall back into the old habit of using credit.

Take a final step forward to build wealth as you _____[27] **for the future.**

This step will be different for everyone based upon your age and retirement goals. None of us know what tomorrow holds. Ultimately we need to look to the LORD and the guidance His Spirit provides. So for now as you think about investing for the future keep these two things in mind:

1. **Don't neglect giving your _____ or making your _____ _____**[28] **debt elimination payment.**

Footnotes:

[26] Pay Yourself First

[27] Invest

[28] Tithe, Step Up

2. **Plan to pay off** _____ _____ _____,[29] **including your mortgage, before retirement.**

We will take a closer look at this final notch in our key to step forward with a financial plan for the future. Carefully cutting this key will unlock the freedom we desire.

The future is going to be here sooner than we think. You can choose not to change and find yourself still in debt, unprepared for the unexpected emergency, and working through your retirement years. Or you can decide to cut the key to your financial freedom. In less than a decade your debts will be paid in full – including that 30-year mortgage. You will have money in savings and what you have invested for the future will begin to grow rapidly – money that was once used each month to pay off your debt can now be added to your investments. With a modest rate of return you could enter retirement a millionaire. Imagine that when you die your estate gives a tithe greater than a year's salary, and your children and grandchildren receive an inheritance that money can't buy. You have left them more than money; you have taught them the principles of Biblical stewardship so they to can live financially free. This is wealth that has the potential to endure from generation to generation. Solomon said: *A good man leaves an inheritance for his children's children, but a sinner's wealth is stored up for the righteous* (Pro. 13:22).

Cutting Your Key to Financial Freedom

Together we have looked at how to cut the key to unlock the chains of debt holding you captive and find financial freedom. Not only will this key eliminate debt, but it will also enable you to build wealth. Remember, God is not opposed to the wealthy. Instead His judgment is upon those who love money. That's why five of the seven notches in your key to financial freedom deal with your heart. They are practical steps that you can take to apply the principles of Biblical stewardship to the way you manage money everyday.

 **Notch 1** You have a new heart because you confess your sin of financial disobedience.

 **Notch 2** You have a thankful heart joyfully expressing praise to God for His provision and help.

 **Notch 3** You have a faithful heart that trusts God tithing 10% of your income.

 **Notch 4** You guard your heart with contentment to step back and stop making impulsive purchases.

 **You develop a compassionate heart as you step out to help provide for the needs of others.**

These five notches will continue to guide your heart and keep you from the love of money so prevalent within our American culture. In this way you can experience God's blessing upon your finances as you cut the notches of the economic matters on your key to financial freedom:

 **You have decided to step up to your debt elimination plan and pay off all your debts**

 **You will build wealth as you step forward to financial stability today and strength for the future.**

Look again at the five heart issue notches on your key to financial freedom? Which one do you think will be the most difficult for you to cut? Why?

Of the two kinds of notches which do you think will be the most difficult for you to cut – the heart issues or the economic matters? Why?

Take a moment now and commit these things to God in prayer asking for His help. Look back at theses again from time to time so you remember to continue to make your need known to the LORD.

notes!

THE THIRD STEP:

STAYING THE COURSE

ACHIEVING FINANCIAL FREEDOM

Unlocking the chains of debt that hold you captive required cutting a key. With its seven notches, our key represents the seven things we must do if we are going to develop a lifestyle of biblical stewardship. This is the key to financial freedom.

Knowing what to do and how to do it are two very different things. This may surprise you, but God is into the details of your life and wants to help you succeed in all your ways. As you trust the LORD with your finances He will show you the way to financial freedom.

> *The steps of the godly are directed by the LORD. He delights in every detail of their lives.* (Ps. 37:23 NLT)

> *The very steps we take come from God; otherwise how would we know where we're going?* (Pro. 20:24 MSG)

In the previous chapter we looked at the seven notches needed to cut your financial key. Five of these focused on heart issues. Don't neglect the notches of repentance, thankfulness, the tithe, contentment, and compassion. Keep these as a matter of prayer; seek the LORD'S help so you will not be led astray. Never forget that the heart determines the path we will follow, whether good or evil (see: Is. 59:12-13; Jer. 17:9-10; Mat. 15:19-20). If you struggle with one or more of these, talk with your pastor or a mature believer who can disciple and teach you about these heart issues. And above all ask them to pray with you for the wisdom and help of the Holy Spirit.

In the following pages we are going to take a closer look at three of these notches. Our purpose is to help you cut these notches correctly and unlock your finances. Together we will identify some specific steps you can take to better manage your money and find financial freedom.

Notch 4

Guard your heart as you "_____ _____"[1] with contentment to stop making impulsive purchases.

Impulsive buying robs you of valuable financial resources; it's an open drain washing your money into the sewer. The check out counter is filled with things we can buy on a whim; retailers do everything they can to encourage us to make buying decisions without thinking about the cost. This is why we need to step back and

learn to _____ _____ _____ _____.[2]

I call these "chocolate cream stick choices." Thinking about my purchases decision like a chocolate cream stick reinforces Biblical stewardship in my mind and causes me to be aware of three important things:

Is this purchase a _____ or a _____?[3]

Am I just seeking my own pleasure, or is this something I can't live without? God has promised to meet all our needs, but He did not promise to give us everything we want (see Php. 4:19). Giving into our wants diminishes our ability to provide for our needs. Choose to make purchases that meet needs before giving into the endless list of wants.

Could the money be put to _____ _____?[4]

We can never spend the same dollar twice; once spent it is gone. Our supply of dollars is limited, but the things available for us to purchase are seemingly endless. Therefore, it is important to stop and evaluate purchases decisions in view of long-range goals. Would the money be better used toward reaching a savings goal, or as a payment on debt? These are some of the potential better uses of the money we have available at any given time.

Does this purchase have any _____ _____?[5]

The simple answer is, "No;" almost everything we buy only brings temporary pleasure. Some things may last longer than others, but when it is all said and done what will happen to what we purchase? Nothing lasts forever; therefore we need to evaluate our purchases in light of making an eternal investment in the Kingdom of God instead. Jesus said:

> *Do not store up for yourselves treasures on earth, where moths and vermin destroy, and where thieves break in and steal. But store up for yourselves treasures in heaven, where moths and vermin do not destroy, and where thieves do not break in and steal.*

Footnotes:

[1] Step Back

[2] Think before we buy

[3] Want, Need

[4] Better Use

[5] Eternal Value

44

For where your treasure is, there your heart will be also. (Mat 6:19-21)

This is why I make don't make some purchases, so those dollars can be used instead to make an eternal investment. Giving to help support missionaries or to provide food and clothing for children in third world countries is like making a deposit in the bank of heaven.

Find The Money You Are Wasting.

The fourth notch is a heart issue, but stepping back to learn the secret of contentment has some very practical benefits that will help us better manage our money. You don't need another job, or more money. Remember God will always provide enough for each of us. You need to learn to use the financial resources God has given you wisely. That's biblical stewardship.

Your key to financial freedom has two other notches that directly affect your monthly budget.

Notch 3 Give the _____ [6] back to God, this is 10% of your income.

Notch 5 Step up to your _____ _____ [7] plan to pay off your debts (goal is 10% of income).

You may be tempted to think you can't afford to do these things. I can year you thinking, *"I'm barely making it now, so how am I supposed to live on just the 80% of my income that is left?"* While you might think of this as mission impossible, God will help you. Remember Paul's encouragement: **"I can do everything with the help of Christ who gives me the strength I need"** (Php. 4:13 NLT).

What you need are some practical ways to plug the holes in your wallet so you can reach these goals. So let's spend some more time on this fourth notch and stop the money leaks so you have enough.

1. **Stop using credit. Only use _____ or a _____ [8] whenever you make a purchase.**

What are some of the ways you waste money with impulse purchases? You probably don't know. Most impulsive buying is done with a credit card because it is painless and so easy. This thoughtless habit only puts you deeper in debt. Remember studies show people buy up to one-third more stuff using credit cards because it's painless. Using cash will make you think before you buy.[9]

The consumer makes impulse purchases. Few of us would take a match to a $20 bill, but impulsive buying is just another way of burning money. As biblical stewards we want to use the money and

Footnotes:

[6] Tithe

[7] Debt Elimination

[8] Cash, Check

[9] *Taking Care of Business: Establishing a Financial Legacy for Your Family.* Lee Jenkins. (Moody Publishers, Chicago. 2001). P. 94.

resources God entrust to us wisely. REMEMBER: Every financial decision, even impulsive purchases are _____ _____.[10]

Whenever we pay with cash or take the time to write a check we feel the immediate loss of the money we worked so hard to earn. That's one way to guarantee we will buy less because the need must be greater than the pain of loss. The simple truth is that if we can't afford to pay cash, then we can't afford to buy it.

2. Saving money at the _____ _____.[11]

We've all got to eat, so start saving money in one of the places you visit on a regular basis. "Supermarkets have researched you and me – and our shopping habits – over the years, and they know what it takes to get us to fill our carts and empty our wallets."[12] We've all got to eat! Studies have shown that the more time spend in the store the more money you spend; therefore, the supermarket will do everything they can to keep you in the store longer. When you go to the grocery store always go with a plan (a list) and then get in and out as quickly as you can.

Saving money on the food you eat: _____ _____ _____.[13]

Let's start in the kitchen. The prepared foods you buy at the grocery store cost more than meals you make from scratch. Ready to go meals, frozen dinners, or other options may be convenient, but they are costly. If you don't know how to prepare meals, ask a friend, get a cookbook, or search the web for recipes and how-to-videos. You will be surprised how tasty your meals can be at a fraction of the cost.

Next, limit the meals you eat at a restaurant. Eating out has lots of benefits. You have lots of choices, no cooking, no dishes, no cleaning up, but you are paying someone else to do all those things and more.

The average American eats about 18 meals at an average cost of $12.75 each, or $232 per month. But when you eat those meals at home your cost may average $4 per person (or less). That's a savings of $8.75 per meal or nearly $160 every month for meals prepared at home – *per person*. Look at it another way: a family of four would save an average of $35 for every meal they choose to eat at home instead of at a restaurant.[14]

Don't let eating out be a regular habit; it will be a drain on your budget, and will increase your temptation to use credit cards because restaurants it so convenient. Make eating out a special treat and not a weekly (or daily) event. Let these dinners away from home be for a celebration. You can choose what and where you eat and that choice will affect your financial freedom.

Footnotes:

[10] Spiritual Issues

[11] Grocery Store

[12] **Grocery Store Ploys.** http://www.bankrate.com/brm/news/advice/19990402c.asp. Accessed, March 15, 2004.

[13] Fix It Yourself

[14] Trent Hamm. **Don't Eat Out As Often** (10-18-17). https://www.thesimpledollar.com/dont-eat-out-as-often-188365/. Accessed, Dec. 30, 2017

3. Saving money at the _____ _____.[15]

We all need clothes to wear along with other items from personal care to household items. However, the first key to saving money is to learn to differentiate between a "need" and a "want." Needs are necessary; wants are extras. Many times when we go shopping we may be looking to meet a need, except while we are at the store we give into temptation and get some of the things we want. You can save lots of money if you take time to plan your purchases on clothing and other items and then stick to buying only the necessities.

4. Keep Christ in _____![16]

Some families think more about giving and receiving gifts than they do THE GIFT of Christmas; Jesus is the reason for the season. You don't have to be a Grinch to learn to save money during the Christmas season. You just need to decide what is really important.

One of my least favorite Christmas songs has a line worth thinking about: *"He's making a list, checking it twice. Gonna find out who's naughty and nice. Santa Clause is coming to town."* When Christmas season rolls around again do the following:

- Make a list and keep going back to it to keep you on track.
- Remember you don't have to buy something for everyone (even if they were nice).
- Don't forget – you are paying the bill, not Santa. This might even mean creating some gifts in your "workshop" at home instead of buying them from the store.

5. Saving money on your _____.[17]

Your car the second largest purchase you will make after your house, but remember, IT'S JUST A CAR! The vehicle you drive is not a status symbol; a car doesn't make you a better person. You are not stronger, sexier, or smarter because of the car you drive. Your car is transportation; it gets you from point "A" to point "B" and back again; nothing more, nothing less.

Before moving on, let me share the most important lesson I ever learned about the cars we drive. The cheapest car you will ever own is the _____ _____ _____.[18] Keep your car maintained, and when it gets older remember that a major repair cost you no more than two to three months of a typical car payment; that's a lot less than the 36 to 60 months or more for a new one.

6. Saving money on debt and _____ _____.[19]

One of the goals of financial freedom is to eliminate all debt. Until you are finally free of debt, make sure you are not wasting money

notes!

Footnotes:

[15] Department Store

[16] Christmas

[17] Car

[18] One You Own

[19] Finance Charges

needlessly with gimmicks and fees lenders will use to siphon more money out of your pocket. Stop using credit. Pay your bills on time and once they are paid off close the account.

7. _____ _____ [20] on saving money.

We could all learn a few things if we sat down and had a talk with our grandparents about the many ways they saved money "in the good old days." Most of us don't know what a recession or depression really is. I heard someone say, "A recession is when your neighbor gets laid off from work; a depression is when you lose your job." For many of us our grandparents are a part of the aging generation of builders who lived through the Great Depression. They did things out of necessity that they continue to do now even though the need is no longer there. Why do they do those money saving things and what lessons can we learn from them? Learn how to be frugal; it will save you lots of money.

With the dawn of the information age we have a wealth of information available to us through the internet. You can find all kinds of money saving ideas on the web for free. If you don't know how to find it ask your kids and they will "point and click" you in the right direction.

_____ _____ _____ [21] in your financial wallet is critical if you are going to enjoy the benefits of financial freedom.
(For some practical ideas see Appendix #3: *"Plugging the Leaks"* p. 67).

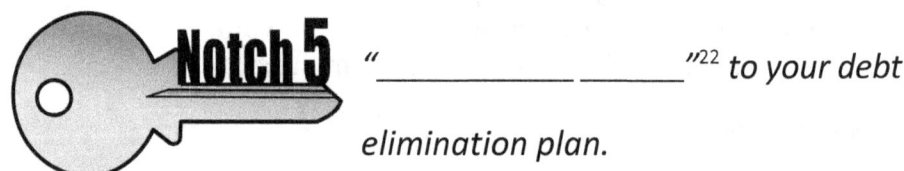

Notch 5 *"_____ _____"[22] to your debt elimination plan.*

You will never be financially free as long as you are in debt. Let the power of the step-up debt elimination plan work for you. As you develop and follow it, you can be debt free in less than a decade – most people can be financially free in as little as seven to five years.

I've earned my MBA from the "School of Hard Knocks." My wife Susie and I have hade more than our fair share of debt: mortgages, car loans, student loans, credit cards, home equity loans, and other special financing options. When I stop to think about it, I'm dumbfounded by the amount of interest payments we have made through the years. But that's the only way we knew how to have a family and provide for all the things we "needed."

I have spent much of my adult life looking for ways to get out of debt. Before developing the step up debt elimination plan I tried lots of other strategies, but none of them worked for us. Looking back at these financial game plans, I've discovered three faulty assumptions that cost us a lot of money. Before looking at the step up plan, perhaps you can learn from my mistakes.

Footnotes:

[20] More Ideas

[21] Plugging The Leaks

MISTAKE #1 Financial Freedom means only getting rid of your

_____ _____. [22]

Early on, we cut up our credit cards and were committed to paying them off. I never imagined paying off all our auto loans; sooner or later we will need another car, which means getting another loan. My hope, but with no real strategy was to pay off the mortgage before retirement. *But isn't debt just a part of life? NO!* Yet with this kind of thinking we soon had opened another credit card account. I knew something had to change; I just was not sure what.

MISTAKE #2 Make more than the _____ _____ [23]

on all your debts.

On the surface this seems to make sense – paying more means paying them off sooner. I had heard financial advisors on the radio offer this advice and had read it in various books. But one day I heard Larry Burkett advise someone like me to pay off your smallest debt; then once it was paid add what you were paying to the next lowest debt and keep doing this until you had paid them all off. The light went on, and I realized I was only throwing money at the problem. It was like the tin cans on the fence, I now had a strategy to eliminate our debt – well at least our credit card debt. And that was actually working.

But we still had a big problem in our thinking. This mistake proved to be the root cause of all the debt and financial bondage we were living with.

MISTAKE #3 All major purchases require a _____ _____

or _____. [24]

Remember the financial teachers we have all learned from? I had learned my lessons well and took advantage of the special financing offers and other promotions available to us. I wasn't thinking about how much things cost. Instead, all I needed to know was one thing: *could we afford the monthly payment.*

That's when I had a paradigm shift - it's a change of thinking you

probably need as well. Put simply, debt is a _____ and not

a_____.[25] I came to the realization that we could

make major purchases without the use of credit cards or financing. Since then we have planned for the purchase of cars, appliances, home improvements, and more <u>without the use of credit</u>. We got off the merry-go-round of debt. This realization and the choices we have made since then have given us a measure of financial freedom. Today our only remaining debt is the mortgages on our home and rental property. These should be paid off in the next five years.

Footnotes:

[22] <u>Consumer Debt</u>

[23] <u>Minimum Payment</u>

[24] <u>Credit Card</u>, <u>Financing</u>

[25] <u>Choice</u>, <u>Necessity</u>

The Step Up Debt Elimination Plan

The step up plan is really nothing more than establishing a family budget. A budget is simply a financial plan; it's a road map or GPS for your money to get you where you want to go. *Without a spending plan or budget, you have no way of knowing what happens to your money.*

Some people are afraid of the idea of a budget, perhaps because they think it is restrictive or hard to follow. A budget is not imposed

upon you; a budget is your _____ _____.[26] Instead

of getting paid each month and telling your money, "Goodbye" with no idea where it went, you can begin to tell your money where you want it to go with the help of your family budget.

Your step up debt elimination plan has four parts:

- Your _____ _____.[27]

- Step Up _____ _____.[28]

- _____[29] Your Debts.

- _____[30] Your Plan.

The step up debt elimination plan works! Let's get started and put your plan together now.

Present Income

The starting place of your family budget is to know how much you make each month. Those who have no idea exactly how much they make per month or year dumbfounds me. This is the starting place of money management; it enables you to establish your spending guidelines. We will not spend more than we make. For our purposes we are using "take home pay" or net income; these are the actual dollars you have available for your monthly expenses.

Your income might be more or less, but since everyone is trying to keep up with "the Jones" we will use theirs as an example:

Monthly Salary	$321 x 2 =	$642.00
Spouse's Salary	$1,652 x 2 =	$3,304.00
Part-time or second income	$120 x 52 ÷ 12 =	$520.00
Investment Income	n/a	$0
Other Income	n/a	$0
	Total Income	$4,466.00

The first priority is the tithe; 10% of the monthly income would be $447 per month. Some may prefer to tithe upon gross income, which would be greater. This is a personal choice based upon the

Footnotes:

[26] Financial Plan

[27] Present Income

[28] Payment Calculator

[29] Prioritize

[30] Activate

50

LORD'S leading and your conviction. The second priority to establish is the step up payment goal. This would also be 10% of the total monthly income or $447. The Jones' example shown here for monthly income will be the basis for the examples that follow in each step. Use Appendix #4 *"Personal Income"* to calculate your monthly income on (p. 71).

Step Up Payment Calculator

Perhaps you are still wondering what a step up payment is. Put simply your step-up payment is made up from the money you have stopped wasting from month-to-month. Every dollar you prevent from leaking out of your financial wallet can be applied to your step-up payment so you can quickly eliminate debt.

The step up calculator is based upon you monthly budget. We begin by listing the current spending. Next we establish the plan for how income will be spent going forward. This is the reduced spending based upon your priorities and the leaks plugged where money has been wasted. Finally the step up payment is calculated as the total saving. Here is a simple example:

Category		Present Spending	Reduced Spending	Step Up Payment
Tithe	(Note i)	$0	$447	-$447
Church/Charity	(Note i)	$100	$25	$75
Mortgage	(Note ii)	$795	$649	$146
Second Mortgage	(Note iii)	$285	$257	$28
House Maintenance	(Note iv)	$0	$50	-$50
Student Loan	(Note iii)	$150	$94	$56
Visa	(Note iii)	$100	$62	$38
MasterCard	(Note iii)	$40	$25	$15
Discover	(Note iii)	$55	$30	$25
Store Credit Card	(Note iii)	$25	$20	$5
Groceries	(Note v)	$485	$400	$85
Dining Out	(Note v)	$230	$100	$130
Telephone/Internet	(Note vi)	$110	$49	$61
Cell	(Note vi)	$199	$177	$22
Utilities	(Note vii)	$409	$380	$29
Car Loan	(Note iii)	$425	$403	$22
Gasoline	(Note viii)	$415	$385	$30
Auto Maintenance	(Note iv)	$0	$20	-$20
Insurance	(Note ix)	$215	$188	$27
TV	(Note ix)	$98	$0	$98
Fun (Movies, Etc.)		$125	$100	$25
Miscellaneous		$165	$125	$40
Savings	(Note xi)	$50	$100	-$50
Retirement	(Note xi)	$0	$25	-$25
Total		**$4,476**	**$4,111**	**$365**

Note the formula for the step up calculator:
Present Spending – Reduced Spending = Step Up Payment

Listing your "_____ _____"[31] will be easy if you have used a money management or check register program. However, this step is not required, but is helpful to find the ways where you can plug the leaks and reduce spending. I suggest filling this column in with the average spending for the past three to twelve months. If you have not used such a program, now is the time to get one; it is a tool to help you manage your money (see: Appendix #5 "Money Management Tools" p. 72).

Establishing a "_____ _____[32] is the key to paying off your debts. The planned monthly budget in the above example is the "Reduced Spending" column. Even if this is the only column you can fill in, it gives you a starting place to figure out your step up payment. The difference between your monthly expenses and your monthly income is how much you have available to begin with as your step up debt elimination payment. You can plan your step up payment using Appendix 6: ***"Step Up Payment Calculator (Monthly Budget)"*** beginning on p 73.

Before moving on, let's _____[33] the step up payment. Notice that the Jones' planned budget in the "Reduced Spending" column totals $4,111. Their total monthly income available was $4,466. The difference between these two is $355, and this is their

_____[34] step up payment. This is $10 less than the projected step up payment of $365. Why did this happen this way? Notice their "Current Spending" column above totaled $4,476; the Jones were actually spending on average $10 more each month than they had in monthly income. Little wonder that even though they were trying to pay off their debts by paying more than the minimum monthly payment, they never seemed to make any real progress. They continually had to keep using credit to maintain their spending habits.

To find financial freedom we must stop the endless cycle of debt by remembering this simple lesson: _____ _____ _____ _____ _____ _____ _____.[35] While we may from time-to-time spend more than our total monthly income, such spending is made from a savings account using income previously made.

Prioritize Your Debts

You might remember that the proverbial light bulb went on over my head when I heard Larry Burkett suggest prioritizing your debts by paying off the one with the smallest balance first, and then working your way up from there. This method works, but fails to give you a target date as to when all your debts will be paid off. I wanted to know how long it would take until I had paid off all my debts. With a little help from a friend, it is possible to to not only prioritize your debts for repayment, but to also estimate how long it will take to payoff each of your debts. That's the method you will learn here.

But first, I need to share one important rule. Failure to do this will cost you money in additional finance charges and late fees. As you begin making your step up debt elimination payment, always pay

the _____ _____ _____ [36] on all your other debts,

and make these payments _____ _____.[37]

So how are your debts prioritized? We will list each of your accounts and apply the following simple equation:

The _____ balance divided by the _____ amount

due, equals the _____ _____ [38] of repayment.

While the actual time is longer due to the monthly addition of finance charges, it serves our purposes. Each debt is prioritized beginning with the one that can be paid off the quickest through the one that will take the longest. Here is how the Jones' debts were listed and prioritized:

Creditors	Outstanding Balance	Minimum Monthly Payment	Estimated Payoff	Priority	Step Up Payment	Payoff Projection
Mortgage	$105,720.^{00}	$485.^{00}	218	8	$1,246.^{00} + $485.^{00} = $1,474.^{00}	61
Second Mortgage	$8,056.^{00}	$257.^{00}	31.5	5	$897.^{00} + $257.^{00} = $1,154.^{00}	7
Car Loan	$8,480.^{00}	$403.^{00}	21	3	$469.^{00} + $403.^{00} = $872.^{00}	9.5
Student Loan	$1,756.^{00}	$94.^{00}	18.5	2	$375.^{00} + $94.^{00} = $469.^{00}	3.5
Visa	$4,450.^{00}	$62.^{00}	71	7	$1,184.^{00} + $62.^{00} = $1,246.^{00}	3.5
MasterCard	$751.^{00}	$25.^{00}	30	4	$872.^{00} + $25.^{00} = $897.^{00}	1
Discover	$1,235.^{00}	$30.^{00}	41	6	$1154.^{00} + $30.^{00} = $1,184.^{00}	1
Store Credit Card	$331.^{00}	$20.^{00}	16.5	1	$355.^{00} + $20.^{00} = $375.^{00}	1
Total Debts	**$151,872.^{00}**				**Estimated months until all debts are paid off:**	**87.5** *or 7.3 years*

The first think I hope you notice about the Jones' example is that **over $151,000 of debt is _____ _____**[39] using their present net income in just over seven years. Like most people I have worked with, you too will see that all your debts can be eliminated in the seventh year or sooner. Again one reason for this is because lenders base how much you can borrow on your present income. I think for those who choose to honor the LORD with their finances there is another reason:

> *At the end of every seven years you must cancel debts.*
> (Deut 15:1)

I don't expect American bankers or moneylenders to obey God's command, but I think the timing for many is the result of the LORD'S blessing for choosing to manage the resources He has entrusted to them as biblical stewards.

Activate Your Plan

Let's look at how the Jones' plan was put into action. You can prioritize your debts and establish your plan using Appendix # 7: **"Step Up Debt Elimination Plan"** on page 77.

As you can see, debts were prioritized based upon how many months it would take to pay them off using only the minimum payment. The "Store Credit Card" was first, which was also had the lowest outstanding balance. However, the "Student Loan" and "Car Loan" were prioritized as numbers 2 and 3, which each had a higher balance than "MasterCard" prioritized as number 4 and "Discover" as number 6.

Once the debts have been prioritized, it is time to _____[40] the step up payment to the minimum monthly payment. Notice how this was done. The actual step of payment of $355 was added to the minimum payment of $20 for the first priority "Store Credit Card," a total of $375. This becomes the new step up payment, which is then added to the minimum monthly payment of the second debt priority "Student Loan:" $375 + $94 = $469. This pattern continues through each debt through the last, which in this example was "Mortgage" adding a step up payment of $1,246 to the minimum payment of $485 for a total of $1,474.

You decide how quickly your debts will be paid off by how much you _____ _____[41] for your initial step up payment.

Remember that the goal for the step up payment is 10% of your monthly income, which in the Jones' example would have been $447. They began with only $355, but exceeded that goal only one month later with the addition of the new step up payment to the

---

Footnotes:

[39] Paid Off

[40] Add

[41] Reduce Spending

54

"Student Loan." If the Jones had made additional cuts to their monthly budget to reach the 10% goal, they would have accelerated the payoff of their debts by six months.

Finally notice that for each debt a _____ _____ [42] is made by dividing the outstanding balance by the new total step up payment of each debt. The total of this column give you an estimate of how many months it will take to pay off all your debts. However, as you put this plan into action you will probably pay off your debts sooner. Why? Remember, as you target each debt for repayment with its step up payment, you continue to make the _____

_____ _____ [43] on all your other debts. This means every month you continue to reduce the outstanding balance on all your debts and avoid additional fees and finance charges. In our example, the Jones would have continued to make the minimum payment of $485 on their mortgage for twenty-six months before adding their final step up payment to pay it off. <u>This means in about two years they have not only continued to pay down their mortgage, but in that time all their other debts have been paid off!</u>

One final note about the Jones' mortgage, which most likely is like yourmortgage as well. If you look at their monthly budget, their "Reduced Spending" amount on their mortgage was $649, but the minimum monthly payment listed on their step up plan was only $485. What's the difference? Most mortgages include a monthly escrow payment for your property taxes and homeowners insurance. Only the principle and interest payment of your mortgage should be included on the step up debt elimination plan. However, be sure to include your escrow payment with all your mortgage payments as scheduled by your lender.

What To Do With The Extra Money?

With the addition of their step up payment, the Jones can pay off their "Store Credit Card" in their first month with $44 left over. Likewise, their second priority "Student Loan" can be paid off in only three and one half months giving them about $250 extra in their four month. What should they do, and in turn, you do when you have extra money left over from your step up payment? Essentially you have three choices:

- _____ the elimination of a debt.

- _____ the extra in your savings account.

- _____ the extra as part of the monthly payment of your next priority debt.[44]

Footnotes:

[42] Payoff Projection

[43] Minimum Monthly Payment

[44] Celebrate, Save, Include

If it were me, I would save the $44 and include it with the extra $250 three months later to take the family on a mini-vacation to spend a day at the amusement park. But here is the point: _____ _____

_____.[45]

What About The Unexpected?

We raised five children, so we understand that things happen you can't always plan for. What should you do then?

Notice two things from the example of the Jones. First, $100 each month is included within their budget as savings. In addition they have anticipated for some of the unexpected in their monthly budget. Previously, nothing had been set aside for maintenance on the house or car. When something happened, it was just paid for without thinking using a credit card. Now an additional $70 each month is being included with their planned savings account for these unexpected repairs. In this way they are prepared to pay cash, instead of using a credit card when the unexpected happens. You can

do the same thing and _____ _____ _____ _____,[46]

like doctor visits and other surprises by including them in your monthly budget.

And don't forget this as well. Your step up debt elimination plan, like your monthly budget, is a guide and not a hard and fast rule. If the unexpected happens, you also have the choice to use money that had been planned for debt repayment to pay for it. Making wise choices like these enables you to use cash and not fall back into the bad habit of using credit cards.

It is time for you to find the leaks in your wallet and stop wasting money. Stop telling your money "Goodbye" and start telling it where you want it to go as you develop a monthly budget and step up debt elimination plan. Until now financial freedom was only a dream, but I hope by now that you can see yourself burning your mortgage. You can be completely debt free in eight years or less.

Build wealth as you "_____ _____"[47] into financial stability and invest for financial strength in the future.

In the previous chapter we saw that we can build wealth in three ways:

- _____ _____[48] to increase your net worth.

- _____ _____ _____ [49] by setting savings goals.

- _____ [50] for the future through retirement planning.

We have already looked at notch 5 in your key to financial freedom. With your step up debt elimination plan, you will quickly begin paying off your debts to increase your net worth. You will be wealthier every month.

Your financial freedom also increases as you decide to pay yourself first. Now is the time for you to intentionally decide to include a set amount of your monthly income for a savings account. As mentioned above, you will actually save more each month than what you budget to pay yourself first. You will also plan for the unexpected as part of your savings for expenses that may actually only happen once or twice a year. For this reason, this money should remain in an account that is accessible and not be tied up in long-term investments.

Initially you might think of your savings account as an "Emergency Fund." As a minimum, I suggest you set a start with goal of at least

$_____ _____ $_____,[51] as this will cover most emergencies.

But don't stop your monthly savings. As your nest egg continues to grow, you might plan for part of it to be used for a major purchase like a new car or home improvement. That's why in time you may want to increase the money in your savings account from one to six months of average expenses. Set goals that you are comfortable with. The important thing to keep in mind is that when you pay yourself

first, you have the power of choice to _____ _____ _____

_____.[52] Paying yourself first sets you free to plan ahead and pay cash even for big-ticket purchases.

The final part of building wealth is to make long-term investments for the future through retirement planning. If you're young think about

waiting to take this step until after your debt is _____ _____

_____.[53] However, you may want to budget a small amount especially if your employer offers incentives to participate in a company retirement account that matches your contributions (never turn away free money); these contributions have tax advantages and are often withdrawn from your paycheck so you won't miss it. If you're older it may be important to begin retirement

savings now even if that means _____ _____ [54] paying

off your debt; just remember to plan for your retirement after your

notes!

Footnotes:

[49] Pay Yourself First

[50] Invest

[51] $1,500 to $2,000

[52] Prepare For The Future

[53] Paid In Full

[54] Slowing Down

debts are paid in full. What ever you decide to do let me encourage you to remember these two things as you build wealth for the future:

- _____ _____ _____ [55] your tithes and

  offerings to guard your heart against the love of money. Remember that five of the seven notches in your key to financial freedom are heart issues.
- Above all, when you begin making investments seek out

  the advice of a _____ _____ [56] who

  specializes in this area and can help you to understand such investments and their tax implications both now and at retirement.

A Final Word

Now it's time for you to take the steps toward financial freedom. You can do it as you choose to:

- **Step Back** to not only think about your finances, but more importantly keep your heart in check to not let money become a rival god that will lead you astray.
- **Step Out** to give of your tithes and offering, not just thinking about yourself, but ready to share and help meet the needs of others.
- **Step Up** to develop your debt elimination plan and put it into action.
- **Step Forward** to pay yourself first and invest for the future to enjoy your retirement years.

Let me finish with my prayer for you and your family:

LORD, I first want to thank you for each of those who have taken these initial steps on their journey to financial freedom. Give each one wisdom to be a faithful steward of what You have entrusted to them.

Thank You LORD, that You are gracious and full of mercy. You have forgiven us for our poor stewardship in the past; I pray that we will experience a deep awareness of Your abundant love and grace. And may You LORD, give us all a heart of contentment in order that we might find the great gain that is ours in You.

Give your children a fresh start. Help them LORD, to apply the principles of Biblical stewardship to their daily lives; help them to change their spending habits in order to honor You knowing that every financial decision is a spiritual decision. Help them to see a preferable future when they are completely free from all debt. Provide each one with the power, perseverance and patience to follow their plan to financial freedom.

In the Strong Name of Jesus, Amen!

Footnotes:

[55] Continue To Give

[56] Financial Advisor

Your Action Plan

- I will read **"Plugging the Leaks"** and make a list of 10 or more ways we can begin to stop wasting money by _____ *(See Appendix #2, p. 62).*

Date

- I will complete my **"Personal Income"** and set my first priority to give my tithes and offerings as well as establish my step up payment goal no later than: _____ *(See Appendix #4, p. 71).*

Date

- If I do not have a money management program or check register, I will get one and begin using it by: _____ *(See Appendix #5, p. 72).*

Date

- I will complete my **"Step Up Payment Calculator (Monthly Budget)"** and verify my initial step up payment through reduced spending and comparing my monthly expenses with my monthly income by: _____ *(See Appendix #6, p. 73).*

Date

- I will complete my **"Step Up Debt Elimination Plan"** to prioritize my debts and calculate the step up payments for each of my debts by: _____ *(See Appendix #7, p.77).*

Date

- I will be debt free and enjoying financial freedom by _____

Date

(See Appendix #7, p.77 – Total the projected payoff months to estimate your financial freedom date).

Signed: _____

INCOME IN THE UNTIED STATES

Median Household Income (2016)[1]

All Households	$57,617	Household Income by age	
White	$61,349	Under 25 years	$30,524
Black	$38,555	25 to 44 years	$62,815
Asian	$80,720	45 to 64 years	$69,822
Hispanic	$46,882	65 years and older	$42,113

Median Personal Income by Education Achieved (2016)[2]

	Less than 9th Grade Education	Non-Graduate (9th - 12th)	High School Graduate or GED	Some College	Associate Degree	Bachelor Degree	Master's Degree	Professional Degree	Doctoral Degree
Everyone	$29,975	$26,733	$36,702	$37,761	$44,511	$67,267	$82,531	$134,719	$125,586
Male	$33,923	$31,682	$43,534	$45,312	$53,571	$82,089	$99,001	$160,528	$151,019
Female	$22,169	$19,052	$27,242	$29,812	$35,559	$52,461	$68,518	$101,939	$90,487
White	$29,838	$27,771	$38,326	$39,110	$45,721	$68,538	$83,161	$135,497	$123,628
Black	$30,944	$22,362	$30,131	$32,938	$38,575	$57,409	$68,613	$121,329	$129,652
Hispanic	$29,140	$29,381	$34,757	$33,756	$38,711	$53,283	$74,412	$101,139	$96,261
Asian	$26,061	$30,427	$32,548	$35,569	$42,382	$68,610	$92,286	$141,615	$134,574

[1] **Household Income: 2016.** https://www.census.gov/content/dam/Census/library/publications/2017/acs/acsbr16-02.pdf. Assessed, Dec. 18, 2016.

[2] **Personal Income: 2016 - PINC-04.** *Educational Attainment--People 18 Years Old and Over, by Total Money Earnings, Work Experience, Age, Race, Hispanic Origin, and Sex.* https://www.census.gov/data/tables/time-series/demo/ income-poverty/cps-pinc/pinc-04.html#par_textimage_12. Accessed Dec. 20, 2016. (Note: The US Census Bureau provides far more information on personal income than what is shown here; I used the "Characteristic: Total" shown on each report which is the median income for all age categories. The following Excel Reports were selected to create the above table: Both Sexes: All Races, Male: All Races, Female: All Races, Both Sexes: White Alone, Both Sexes: Black Alone, Both Sexes: Hispanic (any race), and Both Sexes: Asian Alone.)

LIVING GIVING PRINCIPLES

As the Pastor at Life Church Assembly of God, I encouraged people to think about their finances every week for nineteen years as we received the tithes and offering (notice we received the offering – it was not "taken"). Our giving is a reflection of our hearts, as I often said, *"Show me how you spend your money, and I'll show you the priorities of your life."* The attitudes we have toward giving to the LORD will affect how we handle finances in every other area of our lives.

In time I developed these principles that church leaders other and I would share from week to week. These "Living Giving Principles" helped people better understand how their giving to God impacts their day-to-day lives because every financial decision is a spiritual issue.

Principle #1:   Give yourself to God first.

I [Paul] was there and saw it for myself. They gave offerings of whatever they could – far more than they could afford! – pleading for the privilege of helping out in the relief of poor Christians. This was totally spontaneous, entirely their own idea, and caught us completely off guard. What explains it was that they had first given themselves unreservedly to God and to us. The other giving simply flowed out of the purposes of God working in their lives. (2 Corinthians 8:3-5 MSG)

Principle #2:   Transfer ownership to God, the rightful owner of it all.

David praised the Lord in the presence of the whole assembly, saying, "Praise be to you, O LORD, God of our father Israel, from everlasting to everlasting. Yours, O Lord, is the greatness and the power and the glory and the majesty and the splendor, for everything in heaven and earth is yours. Yours, O Lord, is the kingdom; you are exalted as head over all. Wealth and honor come from you; you are the ruler of all things. In your hands are strength and power to exalt and give strength to all. Now, our God, we give you thanks, and praise your glorious name. But who am I, and who are my people, that we should be able to give as generously as this? Everything comes from you, and we have given you only what comes from your hand."
(1 Chronicles 29:10-14)

Principle #3:   The tithe belongs to the LORD. The first 10% of my income does not belong to me but to God.

"Begin by being honest. Do honest people rob God? But you rob me day after day. "You ask, 'How have we robbed you?' "The tithe and the offering – that's how! And now you're under a curse – the whole lot of you – because you're robbing me. Bring your full tithe to the Temple treasury so there will be ample provisions in my Temple.

Test me in this and see if I don't open up heaven itself to you and pour out blessings beyond your wildest dreams. (Malachi 3:8-10 MSG)

Principle #4: Obedience in giving brings God's blessing on the rest. The 90% the LORD entrusts to us goes further than keeping it all for myself.

Bring the whole tithe into the storehouse, that there may be food in my house. Test me in this," says the LORD Almighty, "and see if I will not throw open the floodgates of heaven and pour out so much blessing that there will not be room enough to store it. I will prevent pests from devouring your crops, and the vines in your fields will not drop their fruit before it is ripe," says the LORD Almighty. "Then all the nations will call you blessed, for yours will be a delightful land," says the LORD Almighty. (Malachi 3:10-12)

Principle #5: The blessing of God's complete provision follows your giving.

You Philippians well know, and you can be sure I'll never forget it, that when I first left Macedonia province, venturing out with the Message, not one church helped out in the give-and-take of this work except you. You were the only one. Even while I was in Thessalonica, you helped out—and not only once, but twice. Not that I'm looking for handouts, but I do want you to experience the blessing that issues from generosity. And now I have it all—and keep getting more! The gifts you sent with Epaphroditus were more than enough, like a sweet-smelling sacrifice roasting on the altar, filling the air with fragrance, pleasing God no end. You can be sure that God will take care of everything you need, his generosity exceeding even yours in the glory that pours from Jesus. (Philippians 4:15-19 MSG)

Principle #6: God will direct my giving above the tithe to provide for a place of worship.

The LORD said to Moses, "Tell the Israelites to bring me an offering. You are to receive the offering for me from each man whose heart prompts him to give. These are the offerings you are to receive from them: gold, silver and bronze; blue, purple and scarlet yarn and fine linen; goat hair; ram skins dyed red and hides of sea cows; acacia wood; olive oil for the light; spices for the anointing oil and for the fragrant incense; and onyx stones and other gems to be mounted on the ephod and breastpiece. Then have them make a sanctuary for me, and I will dwell among them. (Exodus 25:1-8)

Principle #7: Giving is better than getting.

I have not coveted anyone's silver or gold or clothing. You yourselves know that these hands of mine have supplied my own needs and the needs of my companions. In everything I did, I showed you that by this kind of hard work we must help the weak, remembering the words the LORD Jesus himself said: 'It is more blessed to give than to receive.'" (Acts 20:33-35)

Principle #8: **It's not the amount that counts but a heart ready and willing to give all I have to God.**

Just then he looked up and saw the rich people dropping offerings in the collection plate. Then he saw a poor widow put in two pennies. He said, "The plain truth is that this widow has given by far the largest offering today. All these others made offerings that they'll never miss; she gave extravagantly what she couldn't afford — she gave her all!"
(Luke 21:1-4 MSG)

Principle #9: **You can't out give God. You will reap more than what you sow.**

Remember this: Whoever sows sparingly will also reap sparingly, and whoever sows generously will also reap generously. Each man should give what he has decided in his heart to give, not reluctantly or under compulsion, for God loves a cheerful giver.
(2 Corinthians 9:6-7)

Give away your life; you'll find life given back, but not merely given back — given back with bonus and blessing. Giving, not getting, is the way. Generosity begets generosity."
(Luke 6:38 MSG)

Principle #10: **The greater my love for Jesus the deeper my level of giving.**
Level 1. **Obedience.** *Level 2.* **Faith.** *Level 3.* **Sacrifice.**

Since you excel in so many ways — you have so much faith, such gifted speakers, such knowledge, such enthusiasm, and such love for us — now I want you to excel also in this gracious ministry of giving. I am not saying you must do it, even though the other churches are eager to do it. This is one way to prove your love is real.
(2 Corinthians 8:7-8 NLT)

Principle #11: **God wants me to learn to give out of what I have because you cannot give what is not yours.**

And here is my advice about what is best for you in this matter: Last year you were the first not only to give but also to have the desire to do so. Now finish the work, so that your eager willingness to do it may be matched by your completion of it, according to your means. For if the willingness is there, the gift is acceptable according to what one has, not according to what he does not have. (2 Corinthians 8:10-12)

Principle #12: **God wants me to share from my abundance to help meet the needs of others. I believe that when I am in need God will use the surplus of others to provide for me.**

Of course, I don't mean you should give so much that you suffer from having too little. I only mean that there should be some equality. Right now you have plenty and can help them. Then at some other time they can share with you when you need it. In this way, everyone's needs will be met. (2 Corinthians 8:13-14 NLT)

Principle #13: Even when times are tough give with thanksgiving to the LORD.

As they bring thank offerings into God's Temple, I'll restore everything that was lost in this land. I'll make everything as good as new. I, God, say so. (Jeremiah 33:11 MSG)

Principle #14: My offering is a sign of peace with God through the New Covenant in Christ. I understand that my offering does not buy my way into heaven, but is secured through Christ's death on the cross.

All who were willing, men and women alike, came and brought gold jewelry of all kinds: brooches, earrings, rings and ornaments. They all presented their gold as a wave offering to the LORD. (Exodus 35:22)

For you know that it was not with perishable things such as silver or gold that you were redeemed from the empty way of life handed down to you from your forefathers, but with the precious blood of Christ, a lamb without blemish or defect. (1 Peter 1:18-19)

Principle #15: Give with the right motive. Seek to please God and not others.

So when you give to the needy, do not announce it with trumpets, as the hypocrites do in the synagogues and on the streets, to be honored by men. I tell you the truth, they have received their reward in full. But when you give to the needy, do not let your left hand know what your right hand is doing, so that your giving may be in secret. Then your Father, who sees what is done in secret, will reward you. (Matthew 6:2-4)

Principle #16: My offering is an act of worship that tells what I believe about God.

Give to the Lord the glory he deserves! Bring your offering and come into his courts. Worship the Lord in all his holy splendor. Let all the earth tremble before him. Tell all the nations, "The LORD reigns!" (Psalm 96:8-10 NLT)

Principle #17: My offering, above the tithe, is an expression of thanksgiving to the LORD.

I'm ready to offer the thanksgiving sacrifice and pray in the name of God. (Psalm 116:17 MSG)

Principle #18: Faithful giving develops a heart of contentment.

I know what it is to be in need, and I know what it is to have plenty. I have learned the secret of being content in any and every situation, whether well fed or hungry, whether living in plenty or in want. (Philippians 4:12)

Keep your lives free from the love of money and be content with what you have, because God has said, "Never will I leave you; never will I forsake you." (Hebrews 13:5)

Principle #19: God blesses those who share with those in need.

Mercy to the needy is a loan to God, and God pays back those loans in full.
(Proverbs 19:17 MSG)

Principle #20: I do not give out of my own abilities, but it is God through His grace that enables me to give.

But just as you excel in everything — in faith, in speech, in knowledge, in complete earnestness and in your love for us-see that you also excel in this grace of giving.
(2 Corinthians 8:7)

Principle #21: Giving demonstrates that I am becoming more and more like Jesus.

For God loved the world so much that he gave his one and only Son, so that everyone who believes in him will not perish but have eternal life. (John 3:16 NLT)

I live by faith in the Son of God, who loved me and gave himself for me. (Galatians 2:20)

Principle #22: As I give I am set free from worry knowing that God will meet all my needs.

And do not set your heart on what you will eat or drink; do not worry about it. For the pagan world runs after all such things, and your Father knows that you need them. But seek his kingdom, and these things will be given to you as well. (Luke 12:29-31)

Principle #23: A heart of joy overflows within those who freely give unto the LORD.

That day they offered great sacrifices, an exuberant celebration because God had filled them with great joy. (Nehemiah 12:43 MSG)

Principle #24: God's blessing rests upon those who give, but a curse is upon those who are stingy.

It is possible to give away and become richer! It is also possible to hold on too tightly and lose everything. Yes, the liberal man shall be rich! By watering others, he waters himself. (Proverbs 11:24 TLB)

PLUGGING THE LEAKS

As you develop your step-up payment plan (monthly budget), one of the keys will be to find ways to save money that you all ready have and apply it to debt elimination. Here are some practical ideas to help you plug the leaks in your family budget.

Saving money at the grocery store:

$ ALWAYS use a list, and only buy what you put on it.

$ Use the advertised specials to help create your list.

$ Use COUPONS. You can easily save 10% on your grocery bill; with practice you can save 3 or 4 times that much. I've read about shoppers who purchase over $100 worth of groceries, but pay less than $10 because of the coupons they used. Look for stores that will "double coupons."

$ Avoid making lots of little trips to the store; use what is already in the cupboard instead of running to the store to get what you want.

$ Buy store brands; not only are they cheaper, but most are just as good as the name-brand items because they are made with the same ingredients. Try shopping at discount markets such as "Aldi" or "Sav-A-Lot." These are stores that specialize in offering store brand products that can save you a lot of money.

$ Leave the kids at home or you will buy things just to keep them happy. Grocers put lots of things out just for your kids to want.

$ Don't shop when you are hungry; your impulses are on high!

$ Shop at a warehouse club for savings on bulk items. You can save on non-perishables when you stock up once a month.

Saving money at restaurants:

$ Save more on the food you eat—fix it yourself!

$ Brown bag your lunch. A sandwich or leftovers can save you $50 or more each month!

$ Eat at home; the typical dinner out will cost 3 to 5 times what it would cost for you to make the same meal at home.

$ Only eat out for special occasions and not for convenience. As you pay off a debt have a family celebration; work your plan, but don't let it become a burden.

$ When you do eat out look for coupons. Even fine dining restaurants offer special discount through coupon books.

$ Drink water; you will save $1.50 or more on each meal you buy.

Saving money at the department store:

$ Shop discount stores like "Dollar General," "Wal-Mart," or "Target." Keep in mind these stores are also designed to keep you in the store, so you will make more impulse purchases, so USE A LIST and stick to it.

$ Shop outlet stores; you can buy name brand items for half the price!

$ Head for the "clearance rack" and you may find what you are looking for at half the price.

$ Shop the thrift stores or second hand stores. My teenage daughters have saved hundreds of dollars on the clothes they wear and no one knows the difference!

$ Watch for the "seasonal" sales on items stores want to clear out quickly. Don't buy now; wait for the sail!

Keep Christ in Christmas:

$ Give Jesus the biggest gift. One way our family maintains our Christmas budget is by not giving anyone more than what we give in our Christmas offering; it is His birthday.

$ Limit your gift buying for your family to 3 gifts. Jesus received three gifts, so why should our children get more than Jesus? This also teaches our children that they can't have everything!

$ Celebrate Christmas AFTER CHRISTMAS. My parents have our family Christmas celebration on New Year's Day; we don't buy any of these gifts until after Christmas when everything is on sale!

$ Share a "gift exchange" with extended family. Don't buy for everyone; put names in a hat and let each one buy for just one.

$ Involve your kids in the Christmas shopping and gift preparation. Our kids were "apprentice wise guys." (St. Nicholas or Santa was just one of many "wise guys" who gave gifts to remind others about God's greatest gift of all. The truth is better than the myth.) When the kids are involved in the process, we are teaching them about how to plan and make a budget. When the time comes they know who to thank for their gifts as well.

Saving money on your car:

$ Never forget: **The cheapest car you will ever own is the one you own!**

$ Whenever possible PAY CASH, this is one purpose for continued savings in your budget so you can plan ahead for major purchases. If you need to reduce your step up debt payment for a few months and make a "car payment" to yourself so you can go to the dealership and buy with cash!

$ Don't buy a brand new car. In the first two years a car loses up to half its value so let someone else take that loss and buy only used cars. You will save thousands of dollars when you buy a pre-owned car – many that still carry the manufactures warranty.

$ Shop the web first to find the best deal on the type of car you want and then go to the dealership. Also consider shopping area private dealers; they may give greater discounts to buyers who come prepared with cash over a financed purchase.

$ Don't lease a car as an individual. Sometimes it is beneficial for a business to lease a car, but for you and me let's not "rent" a car for thousands of dollars and then just give the car back with possible penalties for high mileage and other fees. Buy the car you need.

$ If you absolutely must finance the purchase of a vehicle, then don't accept a term for longer than 36 months regardless of the monthly payment (if you can't afford the payment, then you can't afford that car). Dealerships try to sell the car by the monthly payment and not the actual price of the car; if you say you can afford $500 a month, then that's what they will try to sell you. When you finance a car don't forget that INTEREST ONLY ADDS TO THE TOTAL PRICE OF THE CAR. If you can buy a quality used car for $12,000 why pay $12,000 plus $3,000 or more in interest? Is the car worth $15,000 or more? If it were that's what they would ask for more.

$ Change the fluids regularly and whenever possible DO IT YOURSELF. Why pay more for car repairs when you can do it and save money?

$ Don't purchase an extended warranty. The manufacturers and warranty companies have it figured out. They know when something is likely to go wrong and they know what it will cost. They don't want to help you; they only want you to help them make more money.

$ **Increase your auto insurance deductible to the maximum.** By using higher deductibles you will save hundreds of dollars each year. The insurance companies have calculated the odds of you having an accident. Higher deductibles are the best value for the money. Lower deductibles do not increase your chances of having an accident; they only increase the profit for the insurance company.

$ Watch out for duplicate coverage. If you have an auto club membership don't pay for towing or other hazard protection through your insurance policy too; your just burning money.

$ Remember, a car is only transportation and not a status symbol.

Saving money on debt and finance charges:

$ Never by "credit life insurance" on any loans. Put simply the finance company is asking you to buy insurance with the finance company as the beneficiary. You can do a better job to insure the payment of debts with simple term life insurance.

$ Check your mortgage for PMI coverage. If you purchase your home with less than 20% down your mortgage company required you to purchase this insurance. Make sure the policy is canceled once you have reached the required 20% ownership.

$ Pay your debts ON TIME. Your credit card company will charge you penalties if you are late, or if you go over your limit. Make sure you send your payments in a timely manner.

More ideas on saving money:

$ Never buy "whole life" or "cash value" life insurance. Only purchase an inexpensive term life insurance policy that provides cash to your beneficiary (i.e. *family*) in the event you die.

$ Never throw anything away that can be reused or recycled. You can get paid for aluminum cans and plastic bottles, so cash in! What are you throwing away what someone would pay you for or that you could save you money by using it again? Why use paper plates when you could wash and reuse plastic?

$ Put your clothes out on a clothesline. You will save money on your utilities, AND YOUR CLOTHES WILL LAST LONGER.

$ Go to a matinee or rent movies; don't pay full price at the theater!

$ Find off-season specials for vacations, amusement parks and other fun things to do.

$ Turn off the lights and use lower wattage bulbs. While you're at it, turn off the TV too. If you need some background noise use the radio; it cost less.

$ If you can disconnect the cell phone; are you paying $50 or more just for appearances? Consider a track phone or prepaid no contract cell phone; this way you pay for only what you use instead of a monthly plan. Do you need a smart phone when you have a computer at home? Do you remember when our phone line plugged into the wall? Do you need both a home phone and a cell phone when an answering machine will do?

$ Never pay full price! When paying cash ask for a discount; credit card companies charge merchants up to 3% (or more) to provide "the service." Or why not wait for a sale and then stock up on the things you need?

$ Don't turn up the thermostat; put on a sweater. Open the drapes to let the sun in, or close the drapes to keep it cool in the summer time.

APPENDIX #4

PERSONAL INCOME

Your starting place is to know how much income you have available each month. Use the table below to calculate your _monthly income_.

Income	Pay Rate Calculation Per Month*	Monthly Income
Your Primary Employment		
Your Secondary Employment		
Spouse's Primary Employment		
Spouse's Secondary Employment		
Your Retirement Income		
Spouse's Retirement Income		
Investment Income		
Other Income		
Other Income		
Other Income		
Other Income		
Other Income		
Total Monthly Income		
Tithe: 10% of monthly income		
Additional Offerings above the Tithe (if any)		
Step Up Debt Elimination Payment Goal: 10% of monthly Income		

* Use the following formulas to calculate your monthly income based upon your pay rate.

Weekly: you receive a weekly paycheck

Take Home Pay **X** _52 Weeks ÷ 12 Months = Monthly Income_

Biweekly: you receive a paycheck every other week

Take Home Pay **X** _52 Weeks ÷ 12 Months = Monthly Income_

Bimonthly: you receive a paycheck twice a month (i.e. 1st and 15th)

Take Home Pay **X** _2 Pay Periods = Monthly Income_

MONEY MANAGEMENT TOOLS

A simple money management or check register program will help you better manage your money. It is a tool to help you take control of your finances. With it you will be able to keep better track of how closely you are staying on track to your monthly budget. Your budget is a spending guide to and not a hard and fast rule. With a program like one of those listed below, you will be able to make adjustments as needed. You will also be able to see your progress as you watch the balances of your credit card accounts and other loans go down.

You can find a wide variety of check register programs using your app store, or doing a web search. Using your app store provides you with reviews from those using the software and much more. Many apps offer a free version with an upgrade to a premium service.

One option I suggest is **Clear Checkbook.** Their tag line says it all: "Money Management Made Easy." You can sign up for free, which give you access to an the following tools:

- **Account Dashboard** – your finances at a glance.
- **Reports** – lets you track your spending and saving.
- **Checkbook Balancing** – the old fashioned register updated to the modern age.
- **Recurring Transactions** – let's you schedule transactions and reminders.
- **Bill Tracker** – keeps track of bills paid and those due soon.
- **Budgets** – set spending limits for to help you get a grip on your finances.
- **Debt Snowball Plan** – similar to the step up pan, this plan that has you pay off your lowest balances first and then roll the money from those payments into your higher balances after they're paid off.

What I like about their system is it operates "in the cloud." Regardless of what device I'm using, computer, tablet or smartphone, syncing is automatic, so I can pick up where I left off. The cloud also enables both my wife and I to have instant access to our account information anywhere.

You can check it out for yourself on the web at https://www.clearcheckbook.com.

Please note this is not an endorsement of their services, but only a suggestion based upon my personal use.

STEP UP PAYMENT CALCULATOR (MONTHLY BUDGET)

The step up payment calculator is your monthly budget. You can use it to determine how much of your monthly income (or take home pay) will be available to apply to your debt repayment. This is done in four steps:

- First, look through the list of categories. Take note of those you use regularly and also look for those where you might have a leak in your spending. At the bottom of the category list you will find several blank lines for you to fill in any regular spending not included on our list.

- Second, use your check register or money management program to list your "Present Spending." Produce a report for the past three to twelve months and enter the average monthly spending for each category. If you don't have such a program I suggest that you do your best to estimate your current spending habits. Enter the total this column at the bottom.

- Now it is time for you to plug the leaks to cut back on your monthly spending wherever possible; enter this amount in the "Reduced Spending" column. This is your new monthly budget. Make sure to include those unexpected items; this money will be added to you're the amount you budget each month to put into your savings account as an "emergency fund." Doing this helps you be prepared, so you can pay cash instead of using a credit card. Enter the total for this column at the bottom.

- Finally, calculate the savings for each category. "Present Spending" minus "Reduced Spending" equals the "Step Up Payment." Enter the difference in the final column and then total this column at the bottom. *Remember, this is your Estimated step up payment; be sure to verify finding the difference between your Monthly Income and the total Reduced Spending Column. Enter your verified step up payment below the table.*

  - Remember, if you are unable to enter "Present Spending" just focus on the "Reduced Spending" column. Knowing your current expenses helps you to find the places where you are wasting money. Again the "Reduced Spending" column is your new monthly budget. The difference between your monthly income and your monthly expenses is your step up payment that you will use to begin repaying your debts.

Take the time necessary to complete your monthly budget so you don't miss anything and you have plugged the leaks. Remember, your budget is a guideline and you can make any needed adjustments along the way.

Step Up Payment Calculator: Your Monthly Budget

Category	Present Spending	Reduced Spending	Step Up Payment
Tithe			
Other Offerings			
Charity			
Savings: "Emergency Fund"			
Savings: Retirement			
Savings:			
Mortgage: Principle and Interest			
Mortgage: Escrow			
Home Equity Loan (2nd Mortgage)			
Personal Loan			
Student Loan			
Student Loan			
Student Loan			
Auto Loan			
Auto Loan			
Auto Loan			
Credit Card:			
Credit Card:			
Credit Card:			
Credit Card:			
Credit Card:			
Auto: Maintenance			
Auto: Gasoline			
Auto: Club			
Child Care			
Clothing			
Computer			
Education: Books			
Education: Fees			
Education: Tuition			
Education:			
Entertainment: Theater			
Entertainment: Events			
Entertainment:			
Food: Groceries			
Food: Restaurants			
Gifts: Birthdays			
Gifts: Christmas			
Gifts: Other			
House: Appliances			

House: Association Fee			
House: Lawn Care			
House: Maintenance			
House:			
Insurance: Life			
Insurance: Homeowners			
Insurance: Auto			
Insurance: Health			
Insurance:			
Insurance:			
Laundry			
Leisure: Health Club			
Leisure: Movie Rental			
Leisure:			
Pet: Food/Care			
Taxes: Federal			
Taxes: State			
Taxes: Local			
Taxes:			
Subscriptions: Magazine			
Subscriptions: Online			
Subscriptions: Video			
Subscriptions:			
Subscriptions:			
Utilities: Telephone			
Utilities: Cell Phone			
Utilities: Internet			
Utilities: TV (Satellite, Cable)			
Utilities: Electric			
Utilities: Natural Gas			
Utilities: Water/Sewer			
Utilities: Trash Disposal			
Vacation: Family Fun			
Vacation: Lodging			
Vacation: Travel			
Vacation:			
Other:			
Other:			
Other:			
Other:			
Other:			
Other:			
TOTAL:			

My Verified Step Up Payment: $_____

Step Up Debt Elimination Plan

Complete the following table. If needed review instructions p. 52-53

My Beginning Step Up Debt Elimination Payment: $_____

① List All Creditors	② Outstanding Balance	③ Minimum Monthly Payment	④ Estimated Payoff ② ÷ ③	⑤ Priority Order column ④ from lowest to highest	⑥ Step-Up Payment Add your step up to ③ of # 1 priority Add total step-up of priority #1 to #2; #2 to #3 and so on	⑦ Payoff Projection ② ÷ ⑥
Add column #2 **Total Debt:**			Add column #7 **Estimated months until debt free:**			

Peter Pan had a shadow like no one else – disconnected and free to do its own thing. Our shadows are different. Your shadow and mine is always connected imitating everything we do. Jesus' shadow is the same way; it will lead us to His feet and reveal what He is doing.

The Apostle Paul wrote to the Colossians about the LORD'S Appointed times saying, *"These are a shadow of the things that were to come; the reality, however, is found in Christ"* (Colossians 2:17). We can come to know the Jesus we never knew as the Holy Spirit reveals Him within God's feasts and festivals established at creation.

WE WANT TO HEAR YOUR STORY!

We are excited to share

Finding Financial Freedom: Your Key to Debt Free Living

with you. Please feel free to contact us and share your story how you were able to unlock the chains of debt and find financial freedom.

Need a little help figuring things out?
Be sure to request your excel workbook to help you calculate your monthly income, step up payment calculator (monthly budget), and step up debt repayment plan.

Send your questions, comments or story to:

greg@thefirstfaith.com